FROM ISLAM TO CHRIST

DERYA LITTLE

From Islam to Christ

*One Woman's Path through
the Riddles of God*

With a Foreword by
Kathryn Jean Lopez

IGNATIUS PRESS   SAN FRANCISCO

Cover art:
Antique Ottoman wallpaper design by
Murat Cokeker, shutterstock.com

Cover design by Riz Boncan Marsella

© 2017 by Ignatius Press, San Francisco
All rights reserved
ISBN 978-1-62164-112-4
Library of Congress Control Number 2017932952
Printed in the United States of America ⊗

For my children

The riddles of God are more satisfying than the solutions of man.

—G. K. Chesterton

Contents

Foreword

"Thank God for ISIS."

You do, of course, do a double take when you hear such a thing—especially when it is said as naturally as it was by an Iraqi Christian woman being interviewed for a documentary. When I encountered her video testimony as part of an exhibit during New York Encounter, an annual festival of religion, culture, and politics in Manhattan, organized by Communion and Liberation, one of the vibrant movements in the Church today, I was transfixed. She and her family fled their comfortable lives in Mosul when the so-called Islamic State gave Christians a convert-or-die ultimatum.

The reason for the woman's gratitude for radical Islamic terrorists? Before she faced such a dramatic choice, she explained, her faith was lukewarm. *No more.* She actively chose Christ because He chose her—for love and mercy and the promise of eternal life.

Derya Little, who was born in Turkey and raised a Muslim, has also actively chosen Christ and left her homeland. Both she and the Iraqi Christian woman described above have made the same discovery: the pearl of great price, who is worth any sacrifice to obtain. The latter has paid the price by embracing her Christian identity, the former by adopting one.

Little has done the world a service by writing this courageous book. On her journey from Islam to atheism to Evangelical Christianity to Roman Catholicism, we see how the Divine Physician brings a healing balm to many open wounds people live with today: broken relationships, abortion, emptiness, unforgiveness. Her story is one of mercy, written as a witness to and an act of mercy.

It's a testimony of faith, yes, and it is also an invitation to look people in the eye and hear their stories—to remember that the person next to you in traffic or taking too long with your order or sitting across from you in the waiting room of an auto body shop is a person with a history and a present and a future, a person who might just have some wisdom to download. It reminds us that the tender love of God in Jesus Christ can be a tremendous leaven for good, not only in individual lives but in society as a whole—and that is why Christianity must survive alongside Islam in the Middle East and be lived boldly and confidently and joyfully here in the United States, where Little and her growing family now make their home.

Let Little's story inspire you out of lukewarm living. She chooses to love, and radically so, with sainthood as the goal for her and the little ones over whom God gave her stewardship. We can and should make the same choice, again and again, every moment of our lives; that is, to answer Christ's call to us. Christianity isn't a lifestyle choice, but the transformation of life. And if we live it, it will show, to the benefit of every person in our lives, and the world.

Derya Little does more than a little to reawaken us to the knowledge that we are beloved by God and have the greatest treasure of all—Christ Himself, who will make good on His promise to bring to fulfillment the saving work He has begun in us.

—Kathryn Jean Lopez
Senior Fellow at the
National Review Institute
April 4, 2017

Acknowledgments

All names, including my own, have been replaced with pseudonyms. I therefore hope that those who have helped me in this journey will know who they are in this story, and I thank them for all of their love and patience. I especially thank Therese, Alan, and my wonderful husband for their invaluable help. I am always in need of more sense.

Turkey, Land of My Birth

As I sat on the white plastic chair at a mechanic's garage in southwestern Pennsylvania, smelling the engine grease and hearing the various bangs and hisses that filled the air, I appreciated the rare pleasure of enjoying a good book. At the time I was a mother of three children under the age of five, and reading fiction was sometimes difficult to reconcile with my responsibilities. Thanks to our busted catalytic converter, there I was, slowly reading the last book of my beloved Dean Koontz character Odd Thomas, enjoying cold, sweet hazelnut coffee, and feeling blessed and grateful.

Looking up from my book, I saw a big wooden crucifix that should have seemed out of place in the mostly metal garage, but Christ's crucified figure did not appear to mind His surroundings at all. I pondered the image that changed everything for me; then I smiled. The reason for my amusement was that if my twenty-year-old self were to occupy my thirty-four-year-old body momentarily, and saw who I was, she would think I had gone insane. The younger Derya did not drive, yet there I was waiting for my huge Honda van to be fixed. She did not believe in marriage, yet I was waiting for the mechanic to finish, so that I could get back to my wonderful husband of six years. A decade ago, Derya did not want any children, yet I was the mother of three beautiful and busy saint makers. She had never traveled outside Turkey or been inside an airplane, yet I was living in a small mining town on the other side of the Atlantic Ocean.

Most importantly, that Turkish young woman did not want anything to do with God, yet I was filled with gratitude and hope at the sight of a crucifix in a garage. Little by little, I had traveled far, not only physically but also spiritually. Thankfully, as wise Gandalf says in *The Lord of the Rings*, "Not all who wander are lost."

My wanderings began a long time ago in a land far away. About fifty-six hundred miles to the east of my home in Pennsylvania lies Eregli, the Turkish town where my childhood and bumpy adolescence were spent. Surrounded by the high mountains in central Anatolia, Asia Minor in the days of the Roman Empire, the town was initially named for Heracles, the divine superhero of Greek mythology, the son of Zeus and Alcmene. The name has naturally undergone considerable change, as has the town itself. During the time of Saint Paul, who was thrown out of nearby Iconium, Heracles was nothing more than a village, remarkable only for its proximity to the Cilician Gates, one of the few mountain passes that provided travelers from the east access to the warm Mediterranean coast.

When I was growing up, Eregli was a small city of less than a hundred thousand Turks, who were nowhere to be found near Asia Minor when the Roman Empire ruled those lands. There remain some precious markers from the ancient times, including a Hittite rock relief of a lynx carved on the side of a mountaintop and the vases and other small artifacts that bored us during school field trips to the museum. As in most cities and towns in Turkey, the major residential areas are rows of tall apartment buildings that surround a downtown. The inhabitants live in apartments with two or three bedrooms, unless they are farmers or ridiculously rich. I suppose Turks like being close to each other. Also, constructing buildings with hundreds of apartments is a lot more cost- and land-effective than urban sprawl.

I grew up in this city with my brother, my mother, and for a while, my father, who on winter mornings would drop a capful of cognac into our tea, so that my brother and I could brave the freezing cold during our ten-minute walk to school.

Beginning at a young age, I tried to picture what Allah must look like and then was overcome with guilt and fear for trying to reduce something immortal and all-powerful to an image in the mind of a mere human being, a slave. Even though my episodes of childish curiosity about Allah's appearance did not usually last longer than a couple of minutes, I would spend the following days expecting to be turned into stone at any moment because of my disrespect. Many times we were told that Allah did not look like anything we could possibly conceive and that trying to capture his visage even in our imagination would be utterly disrespectful and sinful. Thus, Muslim painters and artists are forbidden from making images of the Almighty. Many even refrained from depicting Muhammad's face, because his holiness could not be captured, and attempting to do so would only diminish his perfection.

As my brother and I walked to school, I sometimes stared at the boulders resting beside the creek and wondered if they were once disrespectful children like me. During class, I would forget about my impending doom and learn about the world in books written in the Latin alphabet, instead of the Arabic alphabet that was used by my people at the beginning of the last century. Thus went my childhood in a country that seemed to be stuck between the East and the West, between old and new, between ancient and modern.

Turkey is the last nation state that broke away from the Ottoman Empire. For six centuries the Ottomans conquered and ruled parts of Asia, the Middle East, North Africa, and Eastern Europe, occasionally laying siege to Vienna. They united the ever-quarreling European powers to fight against the oncoming Muslim Turks. In the nineteenth century, the empire started to weaken and lost the grandeur of its golden days. After the rise of nationalism in the aftermath of World War I, many states erupted from the weakly held territories of the Ottoman dynasty. Greece, Romania, Bulgaria, Cyprus, Egypt, Tunisia, Sudan, and Iraq are among the countries that were under Ottoman rule until late 1800s. The Republic of Turkey was the last of these nation states, putting an end to centuries of Ottoman dominance.

Even though the founders of Turkey fought against the Ottoman sultan, in order to create an independent state through the treaties signed between the Allied forces and the new Turkish government, Turkey became the successor of the Ottoman Empire. The sultanate was replaced with a republican form of government, and whatever remained from the empire was replaced with a nation state. A new country, a new government, and a new nation needed to be built. Among other concerns, a new identity had to be formed around this quasi-democratic rule, so that the people who had never known anything other than being loyal subjects of the sultan would identify with the new government. In this endeavor, first and foremost, the Turkish national identity would be built on being the victorious descendants of a magnificent empire, and this legacy, among many other factors, would become one of the central components of being a Turk.

The Ottoman history that was taught to me in school was written from the perspective of the winners and doctored to make the centuries of Ottoman rule look just, fair, and prosperous. My textbooks did not mention the slavery that was legal under Ottoman rule. Unlike American children, Turkish students do not learn about the wrongdoings of their ancestors. There is certainly no discussion of making reparations for past injustices or of moral lessons learned from history—other than never to trust infidels.

Another important aspect of being Turkish is being Muslim. After Mustafa Kemal Atatürk, a former military officer in the Ottoman Empire, led the rebellion that successfully resulted in the formation of modern Turkey, he wanted to ensure that this newly formed state would become one of the civilized countries of the West. Within a decade, the citizens of the Republic of Turkey started to adopt Western clothing: Women took off their veils, and men replaced their fezzes with brimmed hats. The Latin alphabet was used instead of the Arabic script. Turkish women could vote before the women in many European countries. These were only a few of the changes that swept through the land during the 1920s and 1930s.

In having to build a nation out of people who were simply the subjects of the sultan, one of the major tasks of Mustafa Kemal and his colleagues was the creation of a national identity under which the new citizens and former subjects could unite. As I mentioned before, being descendants of a mighty empire was one of the main features of the national identity. Through voluntary and involuntary immigration, in addition to natural and unnatural deaths, the religious composition of Turkey became rather homogenized. For instance, during the first years of the newly formed republic, Greece and Turkey agreed upon a mandatory population exchange. Almost all the Muslims living in Greece were relocated in Turkey, and the Orthodox Christians living in Turkey were relocated in Greece. Needless to say, this exchange caused much pain, suffering, and alienation among the people who were uprooted from the lands where they had lived for millennia. But policies such as these led to one of the most homogenized countries in the world. Today, 99.8 percent of Turks identify themselves as Muslims.[1]

Since the majority of the population adhered to Islam, being a Muslim inevitably became another major component of this brand new collective personality. At the same time, however, Mustafa Kemal believed that the main reason the West outpaced the East in innovation and modernization was the East's strict interpretation of Islam. He therefore imposed a reformed, modernized version of Muhammad's religion on the new republic. After successfully suppressing various rebellions that broke out throughout Anatolia, the young Ankara-based government started to promote a watered-down version of Islam.

In this Islam-lite culture, women were not allowed to cover their hair in the Muslim fashion, nor could they wear the hijab. No manner of religious apparel was allowed in public areas, and both men and women were to dress in appropriate European attire. Laicism, a strict version of secularism that promoted the state's dominance over religious affairs, was embraced, and slowly, but very effectively, religion's impact in education and public affairs diminished.

Despite these shifts in the perception of religion in public life, however, being a Muslim remained an important aspect of being a Turk. You were not supposed to be too Muslim, but you were not supposed to be anything else either.

---

[1] U.S. Central Intelligence Agency, "Middle East: Turkey", *The World Factbook 2013–14* (Washington, D.C.: Central Intelligence Agency, 2013), last updated January 12, 2017, https://www.cia.gov/library/publications/the-world-factbook/geos/tu.html, accessed May 1, 2017.

2

Lessons from Childhood

As I was growing up in this moderately but definitely Muslim country, I was not only exposed to social and cultural aspects of both Eastern and Muslim civilization but was also required by my parents to attend summer religious education classes at a local mosque. Most of the time, these camps were fun for all the neighborhood kids. My brother and I would wake up early, do the ritual purification[1] that was required for us to touch the Quran or to enter a mosque, and meet up with our friends outside. The girls would be dressed in maxi skirts, long sleeves, and a hair scarf. Other than our face and hands, no skin was allowed to be exposed. Our hair was to be completely covered. Boys could wear anything as long as their legs were covered. Walking to the mosque and back with ten or so kids was a lot more fun than learning the Arabic alphabet with the goal of reciting the Quran.

The official language in Turkey is Turkish, and it bears no resemblance to any other Middle Eastern tongue. Over the centuries Turks have borrowed many words from Arabic and Persian, but still the language of the Quran sounds as foreign to a Turk as it would to an American. Thankfully,

[1] This was basically the washing of hands, face, and feet in a certain order while reciting specific prayers designed for cleansing the body and preparing to perform holy acts.

Arabic has an alphabet of consonants, and with the help of special markings instead of vowels, in a relatively short time, one can learn to recite the Quran even if he does not understand a single word.

Reciting the sacred words of the Quran is one of the good deeds Muslims perform in their endeavor to get to Jannah, the Muslim heaven. The afterlife in Islam is rather different from its Christian equivalent. Islam teaches that on Judgment Day all mankind will be sent to either heaven or hell. On this Last Day, the world will be destroyed, and all the dead will be raised for the impending trial. In front of everyone who has ever lived, each person's good deeds will be weighed against his sins. If the sins are heavier, the gates of hell await the sinner. But if the divine scale tips toward his good deeds, even a little, eternal bliss is the person's reward.

Judgment Day is described as crossing over a chasm in which the fiery torments of hell devour anyone who falls into it. To cross the chasm and reach heaven and all its physical and spiritual happiness, one must walk across a bridge as thin as the blade of the sharpest sword. There are two notable exceptions to this rule. The first is probably familiar to many in the West: Those who die in the service of Allah will immediately find themselves in his presence and rewarded with heavenly bliss (Surah 2:159). Those who die as enemies of Islam, on the other hand, will find themselves delivered to the fires of hell promptly upon death, without waiting for Judgment Day.

Even though there is disagreement among Islamic scholars over how long a person stays in hell, all Muslims endeavor to tip the scale of the Last Day toward heaven by racking up good deeds. Being able to recite the Quran adds some decent weight to that side, despite the fact that most readers of the Quran are clueless as to the meaning of what they are reading. That is the reason for spending many a sunny summer morning cooped up in the mosque, trying to decipher the alphabet of an entirely different language.

In addition to learning to read the Quran, we were supposed to memorize many prayers in Arabic, and, of course, master some simple theological aspects of Islam. These prayers were from a few lines to a couple of pages long, and memorizing them was especially hard because remembering anything in a different language, let alone one you do not understand, is very challenging. Even after years of learning English and living in England and America, I have a hard time memorizing prayers. I have been a Catholic for more than eight years and have been praying the Rosary for six years, but it took me a long time to say the whole thing without consulting my handy Rosary card. Reciting the Act of Contrition remains a painful challenge.

Good thing my ten-year-old mind was able to absorb long Arabic texts, because I was required to memorize at least a prayer a week and to recite it flawlessly in front of the imam who instructed us.

The imams were usually very serious and strict, and the holy house of Allah was no place for games. The girls and the boys sat on the carpeted floor on separate sides, having left their shoes at the entrance of the mosque. The Qurans or the exercise books were placed in front of us on little X-shaped wooden tables, because the Quran and the sacred verses must always be kept higher than one's heart. They could not be touched by anyone who was not ritually purified or properly attired. In a building with a fifty-foot ceiling, instructed by a stern, unforgiving imam, my brother and I learned our Arabic alphabet and prayers. Of course, as soon as we left, we and our classmates all resumed our childish pursuits, such as daring one another to walk on the mosque wall without falling or being caught by the imam.

Before a Turkish child turns ten, he is normally exposed to

some form of Islamic education, depending on his parents' level of piousness. He is also exposed to the social and political indoctrination programmed into the elementary school experience. Well before formal education begins, Turkish children learn to appreciate being Turks through a healthy dose of patriotism and sometimes an unhealthy dose of nationalism, with a big pinch of Islam.

As children, of course, we did not care about such silly grown-up notions and insisted on enjoying our childhood. My early years were dominated not by playdates, playgroups, and other organized activities typical of American children, but by playing outside with my brother and the neighborhood kids. My mother would tell us not to come back inside until the evening call to prayer was sung at sunset. Naturally, we were allowed to ask for water and snacks, if the nasty creek water and the various plants we persistently consumed were not sufficient to hold us over until dinner.

After my younger brother and I returned home in the evening, we had no video games or other media to amuse us. We owned a black-and-white television that played cartoons only on Saturday mornings. Thus, we turned our attention to our homework, which we did on a little coffee table we used as a desk, and we ate our dinner on a piece of cloth spread out on the floor. Our parents watched the evening news, but we children had no claim to any entertainment as the grown-ups wound down from the day's worries. Before long it was time for bed. It was a simple and happy life.

During the summer, we children spent even more time outdoors. We played in the tadpole-infested creek, building dams and sculpting mud people. We also made good use of the one ball we had among us neighborhood kids. The number of parks or playgrounds was negligible, and the closest playground offered only a very rusty and pokey slide and two old swings, one of which had been broken many years before. With so few areas dedicated to children, in addition to the creek, we made use of the unprotected construction sites in the neighborhood. Collecting bottle caps, finding stray nails, and jumping off unfinished second-floor balconies onto giant sand piles were some of our pastimes. There was no supervision whatsoever, and all of us miraculously survived childhood.

Even though our actual religious instruction took up only a fraction of our time, slowly but surely we were taught how to think and to feel like Muslims. The biggest problem caused by this early indoctrination was the closing of the mind to any and all questioning. We were taught what to think about Allah, Muhammad, the Quran, men, women, and everything else besides. It is a worldview based on fear and the utter submission that results from that fear. Of course, not all fear is bad, and neither is all submission. But when one's starting point is fear, not love, mercy, or grace, this fear becomes the heavy hand that constantly presses down instead of lifting up.

Islam teaches that Allah is the all-powerful creator of the universe. He sits on his heavenly throne and is completely separate and independent from mankind. We all exist according to his fluid and capricious whim. We are his subjects, nothing more. The concept that Allah could be our Father or friend is utterly blasphemous, because we dare not bring him down to our mere human level. In the same manner, incarnation is inconceivable. The idea that the Son of God could be born from a mere woman would drive a proper Muslim to his knees, ripping his clothes and pulling out his hair as before a blasphemy. Allah is fearsome, inconsistent, and utterly unrelatable. A Muslim prays, but he only appeals to an all-powerful king. His wish could be granted, or he could be turned into a pile of ash, depending on the weather.

When this kind of fear is injected into one's conscious and subconscious thoughts from early childhood, it starts to poison everything in life. It builds a wall that is very difficult to tear down. Fear causes a person to accept what is taught without question or reason. For instance, I remember being taught that Christians worshipped three gods, and that the Bible has been altered through the centuries. Any proof? No. The resistance to doubt and questioning grows so subtly over the years that one does not even realize it is there. Muslims are taught to accept as facts that Islam offers the truth and that all other Abrahamic religions have distorted this truth. Neither of these facts is ever questioned.

In a moderately Muslim country like Turkey, life is relatively comfortable and free, so unless something radical prompts a Turk to question his upbringing, he is content to live in the oblivion. In not so moderately Muslim countries such as Saudi Arabia and Iran, one does not even dare to color outside the lines, because the physical and spiritual consequences would be dire. When I read *Price to Pay* by Joseph Fadelle, the autobiography of an Iraqi Muslim who converted to Christianity, I could not help but feel grateful that I grew up in Turkey.

Nevertheless, even in Turkey, the wall of Islam had been constructed all around me, and I needed a hammer to break it down, brick by brick. The Son of God, who I was taught to believe was merely a blasphemy invented by infidel Christians, proved to be the one who later wielded the hammer. But free will demanded that I go through the crumbled pieces of my former prison to claim the truth for myself. The path beyond the wall was challenging to navigate, but not impossible with the help of the Holy Spirit. After all,

Dean Koontz' humble, wise fictional character Odd Thomas was right when he said: "Fate isn't one straight road . . . there are forks in it, many different routes to different ends. We have the free will to choose the path."

Slowly, many forks appeared in the road in front of me during my wanderings. The first one arose before I became a teenager, when my parents got a divorce in a country where divorce was still rare.

3

Gender Roles in Turkey

If my parents ever had a happy marriage, I do not have any recollection of it. My mother was a high school–educated nurse who worked in a hospital five minutes from us, and my father had a knitting and sewing shop, in the days before mass-produced clothing became readily available in Turkey. I cringe when I remember the knitted dresses and skirts I had to wear. My mother worked from eight to four every day. Then she came home to clean and to cook the mandatory three-course dinner. We did not have a dishwasher—to this day my mother does not own one—so there were dishes to be done after dinner in unheated water. Similarly, our clothes required the attention of my mother's hands, because the incredible invention of the washing machine would not grace our home until I was about nine. On Saturdays, my mother would fire up the water heater powered by coal and wood to give us hot water for taking our weekly baths and for doing the laundry. Thus began her hand-washing of the family's clothing and linens after having worked full-time all week.

My mother worked hard, and a hard woman she became. Looking back, I understand her a little better now, but at the time I did not see why she was bitter and miserable all the time. She was going through what many women go through when they are expected to be full-time housewives while working full-time outside the home. Compounding this stress was a husband who was not pleased when things were not done to his liking.

I cannot say that our situation was unique. All working Turkish women suffered a similar degree of heavy responsibility and inevitable burnout. There were very few men who would be willing to share the burdens of housekeeping and child-rearing. My wonderful American husband, in contrast, has taken over the folding of our never-ending laundry, which threatens to become a small mountain each week. The thought of my father folding clothes is laughable. In Turkey there is a clear line that separates the women's realm from the men's. For many Turkish women, especially those who are modern because they work outside the home, that line alienates them from husbands who still have a traditional Eastern mind-set.

The typical Turkish man has been formed by both Islam, which is not known for its respect for women, and Eastern culture, which for centuries, even before the advent of Islam, has assumed male superiority based on biological and historical factors. From the beginning of Eastern civilizations, men were in charge of riding the horse, carrying the weapon, going to war, and earning the bread. Women were in charge of running the house, gutting the chickens, and doing the laundry. Add original sin to this division of labor, and there is nothing mysterious about how male subjugation of women began. Other than fairly rare exceptions, Turkish men are overlords of their families, rather than husbands and fathers.

In Christian culture, the grace of God manifested through the sacrifice of Christ mitigates against the tendency of men to dominate those physically weaker than themselves, in other words, women and children. The transformation of male hierarchy and authority into a form of service, which happened slowly in the West after the spread of the gospel, did not take place in the countries that embraced Islam. Equality before God, regardless of whether a person is male or female, master or slave, was introduced by early Christians, because their Savior had shed His blood for all. Even though it would take centuries to bring this theoretical equality to a practical level, the fact that men and women stand before Christ as equals made all the difference for the future of the female members of Western societies.

On the other hand, starting from Muhammad's life and continuing with teachings in the Quran and the Hadith, women's role in Muslim society and in the eyes of Allah was clearly established as inferior to men's. A woman's place was not nearly as dignified or holy as a man's. For instance, to nullify a man's testimony in court, two women are needed, since a woman's testimony has half the value of a man's. In the Hadith, Muhammad reasoned that women's minds are deficient compared with men's. Consider what this means in rape cases: The female victim would have to provide more than one witness to the incident, because the rapist happens to belong to the intellectually superior sex.

In Islam men have absolute authority over women, as stated in Quran 4:34. In almost all Muslim countries, women's freedom of movement and speech are considerably limited. Driving, receiving higher or sometimes any formal education, talking to strangers, and going outside without a male protector are not permitted in countries ruled by sharia, or Islamic law. As the privileged members of society, men do as they wish with their women. It is the equivalent of slavery.

Instead of fixing the fallen social order through redemption in Christ, Islam reinforced suppression and injustice, paving the way to the abhorrent treatment of women in

Islamic countries. Robert Spencer's excellent pamphlet *The Violent Oppression of Women in Islam*[1] gives an accurate picture of how women are treated in countries under sharia. Practices such as veiling, stoning, polygamy, easy divorce for men, and beating of wives and daughters should make the feminists of the world drop everything and rush for the advocacy of Muslim women, but instead they conjure up imaginary slights against women in the United States. Alas, some battles are not as popular as making sure that the Little Sisters of the Poor pay for their employees' contraceptive pills, which would cost those employees only $10 a month.

All that said, women in Turkey are in a relatively better situation than women in other Middle Eastern countries because of the aforementioned reforms imposed by our benevolent dictator Mustafa Kemal Atatürk. Women in Turkey may do things that most other Muslim women may not, such as driving a car, getting as much education as they want, going out without a male escort, and avoiding circumcision, which is really a misnomer, because the procedure done to women is something very different from male circumcision and is intended to prevent women from experiencing pleasure during the sexual act.

The sex roles and social hierarchy perpetuated by Islam are still present in Turkey, however. In a legal sense, men and women are equal, but in cultural and religious matters, male superiority and dominance still prevail. For example, in many parts of Turkey, women are never seen wearing sleeveless shirts or shorts, or going outside the house by themselves after dark. Women who make eye contact with men are considered loose. Most rape cases are hidden, be-

---

[1] Robert Spencer, *The Violent Oppression of Women in Islam*, Jihad Watch, http://www.frontpagemag.com/sites/default/files/uploads/2011/03/Violent Opp.pdf. Spencer has done immense research on Islam and the Islamic way of life. His works are highly recommended.

cause loss of virginity, even against a woman's will, is one of the worst things that can happen to her. If a case of rape becomes public knowledge, from then on, the girl is considered impure and unclean, drastically diminishing her odds of finding a husband. Shortly after we got married, my husband and I watched *Bliss*, a Turkish movie about a girl who was condemned to death because she had lost her honor—in other words, was raped. Even though he was not ignorant of the tenets of Islam, my husband was appalled at the status of Muslim women after seeing this heartbreaking film.

Except in big cities, women do not go out for a night of fun by themselves, even with other women. Even if she has a full-time job, a wife is expected to do all the housework and cook dinners with several courses. There are, of course, exceptions to the rule. Having been stuck between the East and the West, the Turkish culture has a multiple personality disorder. Urban areas are becoming more open to and tolerant of the idea that women and men are created equal, but rural parts of the country often seem to be stuck in the times of Muhammad. Thus, the majority of Turkish women remain under the rule of men.

4

Collapse of My Family

My mother's life was not that much different from that of other Turkish working women. She was expected to do it all. She tried to do it all. Not having a jolly personality to begin with, she grew bitterer by the day, as trying to be the perfect housewife and the perfect working woman wore her down. One cannot do it all.

Then there was my father, who liked women very much, and the plural form is not a typo. He wanted them to be spirited, joyful, and playful. My mother was able to bring home a paycheck, cook dinner every day, and run a spotless house, but she was not the warm, cuddly, affectionate wife my father desired. How dare she not entertain his ego? So he decided to find a solution to this problem by looking for pleasure outside his marriage.

Mother could tolerate only so many of his entertainments on the side. The number of mistresses and their whereabouts became common knowledge to all. The final straw came when my father wanted to have a permanent mistress, basically a second wife. My mother not so politely declined his offer. There were many arguments and fights. Since divorce was still uncommon, my parents were stuck in limbo. My father was adamant that his deep dissatisfaction with the marriage could be solved only by his young wonderful mistress, who provided him with everything his legal wife did not. My mother insisted that she could bear his affairs as long as they remained secret, but an open relationship would be too humiliating. Stir some serious financial trouble into this mess, and divorce emerged as the only solution to their dilemma; but for a long time neither of them would even utter the word.

My family lived in an atmosphere of tension and constant arguing that turned violent. I kept thinking that life would be much better and more peaceful if my parents finally caved in and got a divorce. I thought that once they stopped driving each other crazy on a daily basis, my brother and I would still see both of them and all would be well. Their marriage had become so noxious that, to my young mind, divorce seemed the best alternative. Sadly, I was naïve to think that divorce would fix my wounded family.

Over and over, my father swore that he would not be the one to dissolve our family. At the end of an evening of breaking windows, ripping clothes, and staining walls with blood, my father took me aside to tell me that he would never abandon us for a woman. But he left our home that night, and I did not see him again for the next five years. I was twelve years old, and my brother was ten. Our parents' marriage shattered into pieces, and the peace I had expected did not materialize.

By the time my father left, my mother had retired from her position as a nurse, so that we could use her lump-sum retirement payout for a down payment on our apartment. Even though she was only thirty-eight when she retired, she opted to stay at home instead of trying to find another job. But staying at home in a culture in which divorced women were looked down upon drove her into depression. Women were already considered inferior to men. Now that she was alone by choice, there was no support whatsoever from my mother's extended family or from my paternal uncles and aunts. She had to become both father and mother for the three of us to survive. It was not just running the household and making sure that the bills were paid. She also had to make sure that my brother and I behaved like perfect preteens. My mother could not bear to hear one negative word about her home or her children from anybody, even if the gossipers were complete strangers. The pressure of having to please the entire town with her housekeeping and her troubled children was too much.

As a form of therapy and escape, she proceeded to crochet day and night on a cushion next to the heater in the living room. She became a physically present but emotionally absent mother. During our school hours, my mother would cook dinner and clean the house so that we would still live in a decent place. But, as soon as she was done with those duties, the cushion next to the heater and the crochet hook claimed the only parent we had left.

My brother and I were still expected to come home not long after dark, but other than that, we were left to our own devices. As parents of preteens and teens will appreciate, this was not a good way to wade into the oncoming storms of puberty. Not having a functioning family to speak of and not receiving love at home, I started to idolize my friends and tried desperately to fit in. Because of my parents' divorce and my own insecurities, I felt like an outcast.

At the same time, the religion I was taught my whole life proved to be nothing but dust. I anxiously said the prayers I memorized all those years ago, fasted during the month of Ramadan, and read the Quran when I felt lost. The more I tried to pour my heart out to the god of my parents, the more I felt as though I was talking to a person who was not there. The more I tried to grasp, the more futile my memorized gibberish prayers felt. I was in a room all by myself, and no one was listening.

In that dark room, slowly the unthinkable seeds of doubt were sown. They were very small seeds at first—so small, in fact, that I was not willing to acknowledge them. But my prayers became shorter and shorter. They were said out of habit without any heart or belief that someone was hearing the incomprehensible Arabic words. Then I started to find excuses to delay reading the Quran. Either I was too busy with homework, or I was not ritually clean. One Ramadan, I simply lied to my mother about fasting. I would wake up before sunrise with her to eat and then pretend to fast while grownups were around. Drinking water and having little snacks when nobody was looking became the way I fasted. By no means had I left Islam, but my adherence became only nominal. I was becoming one of the millions of Muslims in Turkey who did not observe the religion to which they claimed to belong, and I was content with that development.

This disillusionment coincided with my starting to attend a school that accepted only students who passed a comprehensive test administered to fifth graders. The system is different now, but back then I entered our town's most elite school, which all parents wanted their kids to attend. This was mostly because classes were smaller and all the important courses, such as science and math, would be taught in English. Accepted students were required to take a year of intense English preparation.

As I struggled to learn a foreign language that was immensely different from Turkish, along with dealing with a crumbling family, my thoughts and doubts about religion were set aside for a short while. I wanted only to figure out how to compose questions in the blessed English language and sing "Ba Ba Black Sheep" without butchering the poor lamb. Other than wrestling with English grammar, I found myself anxious about trying to fit in with a group of girls in this school. My teenage years came upon me like a storm, and my need to receive from the other kids at school the love I did not get at home intensified.

5

Loss of My Faith

Soon after my parents went through separation and divorce, we slipped down the financial ladder. Money became very scarce, as my mother had to pay the mortgage and feed us with only her meager retirement salary. Seeing all my better-off friends wearing Levi's 501 jeans and buying New Kids on the Block cassette tapes, which were expensive in Turkey, while I had only a battered old pair of shoes and a knock-off pair of jeans, made me feel as if there was no room for me in their world. I felt neglected by my parents and patronized by my friends.

Having a natural propensity to nerdiness, I slowly turned to books. My bedroom, which had been formerly dedicated to reciting the painfully memorized prayers and verses from the Quran, became a sanctuary where I hid myself in the strange worlds of fictional characters.

At first I read Steinbeck, Verne, and shorter works of Dostoyevsky. Not many other kids had the same taste in books as I had and tried as hard as I did not to care about what the rich kids were wearing. But after a while, I found another bookish person to be my friend. She was being raised by atheists instead of Muslims, and she introduced me to the writer Turan Dursun.

Born in 1934, Dursun was trained to be a Shia Islamic scholar. After years of extensive education, he became an Islamic cleric. As he studied the history of monotheistic religions (mainly Islam, then Judaism and Christianity from an Islamic perspective), however, he slowly became disillusioned by Muhammad and his religion. Eventually, Dursun left his position as a cleric and became a writer whose life was threatened regularly by Islamic fundamentalists. In 1990, some of these Muslims decided to make good on their threats and murdered Dursun outside his home in Istanbul. As is common with murdered writers, Dursun had more influence than before: He became a martyr for Turkish atheists, and his books sold by the thousands. I was introduced to this man's work when I was about thirteen, in 1993, not long after his death.

Dursun wrote many books against Islam, but the first two volumes of his *This Is Religion* series fertilized the seeds of doubt in my mind and grew them into mighty oaks.

In the first book, subtitled *God and the Quran*, Dursun laid out the shortcomings and contradictions of Allah and Muhammad. By that time, I had not read the Quran in Turkish, nor did I have the desire to read the numerous hadith, or traditions left behind by Muhammad. In contrast, Dursun had devoted his formative years and a significant part of his adult life to the study of Islam. He had much to say. Devouring his books came easy to me, because after all, I had sensed the emptiness and realized the futility of incomprehensible prayers. I was primed to hear more.

This Is Religion: God and the Quran begins by explaining Muhammad's sexual deviancy and how new verses supposedly sent by Allah happened to accommodate his sexual whims. For instance, at first Muhammad was supposed to sleep with his many wives in an orderly fashion so as not to skip anyone. But then he received a revelation from Allah that he could sleep with whichever wife he wanted. Allah so accommodated Muhammad's carnal desires that if the prophet wanted a woman her husband was required to divorce his wife so that she could be Muhammad's. This divine favor was explained by a Muslim scholar as a reward and an encouragement for the hardships of receiving revelations from Allah.[1]

One of the many other examples of Muhammad's sexual life that Dursun dwelled on, which had disturbed me even before I came to know Dursun's writings, was the prophet's betrothal to a six-year-old child, Aisha. Even though Muhammad did not have intercourse with her until she was nine years old and he was fifty-two, in the sunnah Aisha recounts the day she was taken to his bed chamber, a day she had to leave her friends behind while they played on the swing and the teeter-totter. I felt sick as I read the account of Aisha. I thought about my sweet little neighbor who was almost nine and pictured her being married to a middle-aged man. Instead of finding Muhammad's behavior disturbing, Islamist theologians have reasoned that since a girl of nine could cause lust in a man, nine years old must be a marriageable age.[2] Hence the child brides in Muslim countries. To this day this abhorrent practice steals the childhood of many girls, and it was started and sanctioned by Muhammad.

Muhammad's sexual conduct had many more elements that are repulsive, even in the eyes of our sex-saturated culture. It is easy to find out about Muhammad's life and adventures with women, if one is willing to doubt the perfect nature of Islam's prophet. Muhammad's legitimization

[1] Turan Dursun, *Din Bu 1: Tanri ve Kuran* (This Is Religion 1: God and the Quran) (Ankara: Kaynak Yayinlari, 2013), pp. 10–19.

[2] Ibid., pp. 23–29.

of polygamy, child brides, domestic rape, and rape of women captured during battle were enough for me to take another step away from a religion founded by this kind of man. Another delegitimizing factor was the promotion of violence and jihad in Islam.

Alongside Ottoman history, the history of Islam is taught in Turkish elementary, middle, and high schools. Textbooks chronicle the conquests of Muhammad and those of Islamic countries. They claim that the holy prophet was trying to save stubborn and sinful people by bringing them under the rule of Islam, the only true religion. Islam's expansion was good not only for the new territories that "willingly" came under its rule but also for Muhammad and for the glory of Allah. I do not remember ever questioning whether the people of those strange lands wanted to become Muslims, or in what manner they agreed to come under Islamic rule. Since there was no mention of bloody conquests or forced conversions, we assumed in our childhood innocence that all went smoothly as people joined the Islamic ranks with chants of bliss.

During my teenage years, suspicions that Islamic history was not as rosy as it was depicted in our textbooks entered my mind. Especially after reading Dursun and being slapped in the face with what kind of a life would have awaited me had I been born in a more conservative Muslim country, my eyes were slightly more open to the story that was hidden between the carefully manipulated lines of my textbooks.

Muhammad was raised by his uncle after having been orphaned at the age of six. As an orphan, he was not the favorite member of the clan, since he was perceived as weak. Later in life, he started to retreat into caves in the mountains alone for weeks at a time. One day when he was forty years old, he came out of the caves claiming that he had had an encounter with Cebrail, the Angel Gabriel, and was given the first verses of the Quran. As he supposedly continued to receive revelations from Allah, he started to share these encounters with those around him. Three years after the reception of his first verse, in 613, Muhammad started to preach publicly.

At first, he condemned polytheism and idol worship, which were rampant in the Arabian peninsula. As the leadership of his clan changed and his safety in Mecca, his hometown, came into question, Muhammad and his followers migrated to Medina, facing little opposition there. In this new city, he laid the foundations of the first Islamic state. A conflict erupted between the followers of Muhammad and the Meccans who opposed his teachings. Soon thereafter Muhammad delivered verses that allowed the raiding of Meccan caravans, resulting in the increase of wealth and power of Muhammad's followers.

When Muhammad and his then small army defeated the Medina forces, killing many of the leaders despite being outnumbered three to one, the opposition to Muhammadan teaching diminished. A few pagan opponents were murdered for their outspokenness, and their murders went unpunished. As he established his position in Medina, Muhammad started to expel the Jewish tribes of the city and claimed their remaining properties. His followers grew in number and viciousness. Slowly, with overwhelming force and the advantage of surprise, Muhammad conquered many Arabian tribes.

After enjoying two peaceful years in Medina, Muhammad gathered the strength and the numbers to conquer Mecca. With tens of thousands of Muslim converts on his side, he seized Mecca with little loss. Most Meccans converted to Islam, and all the statues of the local idols were destroyed.

In his later years, Muhammad fought in battle after battle to suppress those who wanted to end the reign of the Islamic state. He died in A.D. 632, after spreading Islam throughout the Arabic world in mere decades.

In book after book I read about Muhammad's life. Since the naïveté and the submission of my previous years had left me long ago, I understood that not all who converted to Islam had the option to refuse. For many, it was a choice between life and death. If people were convicted enough to hold on to their own beliefs, such as the Jews of Mecca, available options under Islam were exile, alienation, and many times the bloody edge of the sword. Muhammad could never claim that the killing he did and the wars he waged were for self-defense. He became a warrior through and through, craving power over men and women alike.

It was hard to believe that I had been completely blinded to the truth that Muhammad was yet another power-hungry man who was willing to do whatever it took to expand his empire. He did this in such a clever, masterful way that the religion he established spread like fire as the swords he blessed chopped the heads of rebels and resisters. Through the use of violence he convinced many thousands of people that it was truly advantageous to do Allah's will, as he interpreted it, since the converted reaped rewards both in this world and in the next.

The veil was lifted. After having read these accounts with fresh eyes, I was appalled at how so many people, including myself, could blindly follow this man. He was not much worse than many kings, emperors, or sultans as far as his military affairs were concerned, but his claim to having been entrusted with bringing the one and only religion to the people was reprehensible. How could I follow a man who had no conscience? Muhammad not only wielded the sword, but also approved and encouraged the use of force to expand the kingdom of Allah. The verses the Angel Gabriel supposedly brought him varied according to his political agenda. As the Islamic state grew, Muhammad's power, wealth, and influence reached new heights. He claimed what he wanted for himself.

If this was what the founder and the leader of Islam did, what type of atrocities would his followers be capable of? Just like everybody in America, I vividly remember where I was and what I was doing on the fateful day when two commercial airplanes were flown into the World Trade Center full of civilians. It was five in the afternoon in Turkey, and I was helping to take inventory in a Christian bookstore as it was getting ready for its grand opening in a few weeks. At that time, I was not a Christian and did not have any intention of becoming one. But since I could speak and write English, I helped to enter the English-language books in the inventory. During my coffee break, someone rushed into the room, breathless from running, and said that America was under attack. He briefly described what had happened and urged me to join the others watching the news.

I could not believe my eyes—not because I could not imagine people capable of such an atrocity, but because I could not imagine how the lone superpower in the world was unable to thwart it. As we watched the clip of towers collapsing over and over again, I was half convinced that it was a hoax.

What made me utterly disgusted was seeing people in Muslim countries cheering as they watched thousands of people burn to death or perish under the falling buildings. Having struggled with terrorism for years and witnessed much blood spilled in mindless acts of violence, the people in Turkey reacted differently, even though some believed that Americans brought the attack upon themselves or even deserved it. In my homeland, there was no cheering or applause as we watched groups around the world gathering in front of television screens and clapping and screaming "Allahu akbar!" How could they take such joy in immense pain and suffering?

In my atheist mind, all I could think of was Muhammad raiding trade caravans and sanctioning the murder of his opponents. That was centuries ago, and his views and the teachings of his religion had now ripened into a brand-new kind of violence. It was jihad in its modern rawest form, and it was ugly.

Not every Muslim seeks to destroy infidels. There are millions of adherents of Islam who want to live in a nice house, drive a good car, and raise respectful and successful children. My parents, my brother, my sister-in-law, and my nephew are all Muslims. None of them would hurt a fly, let alone condone acts of terrorism. Unbeknownst to them, however, their religion promotes violence as a means to an end. Whereas my relatives see a way to get to heaven through prayer, fasting, and being kind to others, some read and adopt Islamic practices strictly and have no qualms about killing the innocent. My parents' Islam is watered down. Muhammad's real religion, on the other hand, demands much more than fasting and praying from its adherents.

The worldview of Islam is drastically different from that of Christianity or even Buddhism. There is no distinction between church and state. On the contrary, according to Islam, the religion and the state are intertwined. One's religion is not only an individual affair, but also the glue that holds the society together and the compass that should guide the government. It sounds wholesome and desirable when described as such, especially when modern culture does not offer anything other than decadence. Jesus told Peter to put his sword back into his scabbard (Jn 18:11), but Muhammad sent his followers into battle.

Religion's place in government, according to Islam, is as an external force that coercively shapes the society. The government is to implement Islamic law, sharia, which rules with an iron sword. Theft is punishable by amputation. Criticizing Allah, the Quran, or Muhammad is punishable by death, as is leaving Islam. Wife beating and polygamy are allowed. War to spread Islam through the subjugation of infidels is encouraged.

Christ asks His followers to change themselves before attempting to change others (Mt 7:1-5). Christ showed mercy to the adulteress who was about to be stoned, and He asked those present to examine their own consciences (Jn 8:3-11). This internalization makes it possible for the Christian to be faithful to a secular government. As long as Caesar does not play God, the Christian is required to be a dutiful citizen. It is undeniable that religion functions as glue in a society. What the glue is made of, however, is equally important.

According to Islam, those who rule without Islamic guidance are in an existential dilemma: Either submit to the rule of Allah or be conquered by those who do. Many Muslims think that the world would be better off if everyone lived under Islamic law. Since nothing can take precedence over expanding the kingdom of Allah, all Muslims are required to be part of this struggle that is called jihad. It is a political and religious end, and both aspects of jihad complement and encourage the other. Ottoman sultans often used their religious authority as caliphs to further their political goals. The conquest of Istanbul and other Christian territories was attempted not only because of their geopolitical importance or wealth, but also because Muhammad said that the one who conquered Constantinople would be the awesome commander of a fearsome army.

On the other hand, Saint Peter was not given permission to wield his sword when he tried to defend Christ on the night of His arrest. Following his Savior's command, Peter and those who succeeded him would not wield the temporal sword themselves. The Church of Rome opted to rely on the armies and the soldiers of the Catholic kings. Therefore, a secular ruler can be a Christian, but not a cleric. In Christianity, theocracy is forbidden. The Christian is charged with forming as just a society as possible, always keeping in mind that before God all men are equal—and fallen.

The Muslim is charged with expanding Allah's kingdom by the sword and making sure that sharia is followed. The Christian state may have taken a dim view of apostasy, but Christianity evangelized the Roman world while being persecuted by a pagan state. Thus, coercive conversion was officially forbidden by the Church, even if at times Christian rulers used force to impose their faith upon their subjects. Although it appears that Muslims and Christians have similar moral codes, the worldview and the source of these laws are completely opposite, and this reality renders the two religions incompatible with each other.

In Muhammad's life, I saw blood, destruction, and selfishness, not the acts of a sinless man, as the Muslims claim him to be. I realized that the exalted founder of Islam was only a sinful man who used his influence to further himself. I could not even respect him for his accomplishments. Thus, I completely turned by back on Islam. I could not possibly follow a man so violent and selfish. If there were someone I would be willing to lay my life down for, he would have to be willing to sacrifice himself for me and to promote selflessness and peace instead of chasing after the pleasures of this world. As far as I knew, there was no such man.

After Muhammad's time, the reign of bloodshed did not diminish. Muslim leaders continued to wage wars and to subjugate other peoples in the name of Allah. By reading the history of Islam from the seventh century until the present day, one can see that Islam is a religion not of peace but of submission. Thus, I came to the conclusion that religion was nothing more than an effective way for power-hungry men to manipulate people. There was no authenticity or genuineness to be found in any religion, I decided. I whole-heartedly believed that all religions started in the same way that Islam did and likewise evolved into a means to control the masses. I therefore wanted nothing to do with any of them.

6

Islam and Christianity

Although I grew up in a country where violence was accepted as part of life because of the clashes between the Turkish military and the PKK, a Kurdish terrorist organization, I still was taken aback by the bloodshed in the name of Islam during Muhammad's lifetime. I was barely thirteen years old when I learned how Islam had spread during its first few decades, and this discovery destroyed whatever connection there was between my parents' religion and me. I simply did not want to follow a man like Muhammad. It is important to clarify that I did not become a pacifist. Violence, struggle, and fighting were part of Turkish identity. The country had mandatory conscription of every male aged eighteen. Terrorist bombs exploded every other day, killing some and wounding many. The importance of being strong and tough in order to protect our national security was ingrained in us from an early age.

In addition, seeing where meat comes from is a crucial element of being a child in Turkey, and I dare say in any Muslim country. We learn to stomach the sight of blood and internal organs from childhood. One of the two main Muslim holidays is Eid al-Adha, also known as the Feast of the Sacrifice. Most Muslims are unaware of the origin of this holiday, which is derived from Judaism and the covenant with the Lord that established animal sacrifices as a means of atonement for sin. The story of Abraham and Ishmael, who replaces Isaac in the Quran, is widely known and accepted as the source of the tradition (that Abraham's sacrifice of his son foreshadows the sacrifice of Christ is obviously missed). The practice of animal sacrifice is so important that it is one of the five pillars of Islam.

Before or on the first day of the feast, families who have the means to participate buy a sheep, a goat, a cow, or a bull to be sacrificed. Sometimes a kid or a lamb is brought to one's property ahead of time and fed by the family for weeks in order to be fattened for the sacrifice. Even though children have no illusion that they would live to a ripe old age with the sweet little lamb, it is never easy to see a baby animal that one has been feeding and bonding with for weeks bleed to death. Thankfully, this trauma happened to me only a few times. Many friends who witnessed the slaughter repeatedly almost became vegetarians, which are practically unheard of in Turkey; we don't even have a word for someone who doesn't eat meat other than "vejeteryan". We Turks like our meat.

As mentioned before, the blood sacrifice is reminiscent of the sacrifices made for the atonement of sin in the Old Testament. In Islam, one can absolve his sins through repentance, almsgiving, or participating in some other good deed, called *sevap*. Muhammad claimed to have established an Abrahamic religion, yet he apparently failed to comprehend the bridge that God had built between mankind and Himself through the temple, the Levitical priesthood, and the sacrifices spelled out in the Mosaic Law. Therefore, as a Turkish child in the 1980s, I witnessed the shedding of animal blood without being exposed to what it signified.

This regular exposure, in addition to the realization that

life is utterly fleeting because of the all-too-frequent bomb-
ings and armed conflicts, meant that we were no strangers
to violence. The United States is unique and blessed not to
have borders with many countries. Having vast bodies of
water on either side of one's country gives a sense of security, even if it has been slowly diminishing since 9/11. Turks
have never had that relative peace of mind. Bordering Iran,
Iraq, Syria, and, at one point, the Soviet Union, the country
has always felt vulnerable. The Turkish government and the
military have always played on the people's fear of invasion.
Some of the threat has been real, and some imagined, but
there has always appeared to be some existential peril, or so
we were taught to believe. We have been trained to sacrifice ourselves to defend our country if needed. Our parents
and teachers made sure to instill in us that there are more
important things than one's personal life and dreams.

Despite being exposed to the reality of violence and death,
the more I read about Muhammad and his religion, the more
I wanted to run in the other direction. At that time, I did
not know what the other direction was. All I could do with
my new understanding was denounce Islam and get on with
my life.

Losing my religion, as the band R.E.M. puts it, naturally
led to a change in lifestyle. I was barely a teenager when
I started to break away from any form of moral compass.
Although Islam did not always point in the direction of true
north, dropping the only needle I ever had left me defense-
less against the angst and the hormones of my adolescent
years. Soon enough, I surrounded myself with other kids
from troubled families who were also disinclined toward
any faith. As time passed and I lost the fear and the attachment to Islam that was ingrained in me from childhood, I
became more and more drawn to atheism.

During high school, I read a little from the Gospels out of

curiosity, but by then my cynicism about all religions had calloused my heart. As I said before, when I rejected Islam, I put all other religions in the same category as the violent, antiwoman, political ideology Muhammad promoted. To me, Islam and Christianity were different chapters of the same book.

Yet there was another reason for my negative attitude toward Christianity: those summers learning about Islam in the neighborhood mosque. There I was instructed that Allah had sent Muhammad because the Christians had deviated from Allah's original plan, changed the Bible, and equated Jesus with God. Muhammad was sent to put an end to this heresy and to bring Allah's original plan to fruition. Despite the fact that I rejected almost everything that I was taught in my religious education, I subconsciously accepted that Christianity was corrupt and full of unending lies. Although I discarded everything Islam declared as truth, I did not stop to consider what Muslim scholars claimed to be false. In those years, it did not even occur to me to doubt Islam's teaching about Christ and the Bible.

Turkish children are inoculated against Christianity not only at the mosque but also at the theater. In Turkish movies set during the Ottoman era, all bad guys are Christians. These infidels commit many atrocities against the innocent. The audience can be sure that somebody is about to be raped or tortured whenever a soldier with a cross painted across his chest enters the scene. Nothing is worse than when the Crusaders show up. The bloodthirsty soldiers of Christ steal everything in their way, rape every woman they meet, and for good measure burn every village they enter. On the other hand, all the Turks do is defend their holy lands. From an early age Turks are taught that Christians are bad guys and that we Muslims should be united against them—not all

Muslims, however. According to us Turks, some Muslims are better than others.

Turks are not sexist enough to think that only Christian men were malevolent back in the days of the Byzantines. Christian women could be worse. In our films, they dress immodestly in order to seduce men, especially brave, virtuous Turkish soldiers. The women of the West are shown to be skilled at conspiring and conniving—experts at various crafty means of murder, such as poisoning. Cersei or Margaery in *Game of Thrones* would have been apprentices under these mostly Byzantine, occasionally German, Christian women. The rare gem who is portrayed as a moral Christian lady inevitably falls in love with the protagonist and converts to Islam. But such virtue is always the exception. After watching about a hundred of these movies and killing plenty of imaginary Crusaders at the end of stick swords with the neighborhood kids, it is very hard to see Christianity as anything other than evil.

The combination of school, mosque, and theater, along with the complete lack of practicing Christians in my region, resulted in my not going anywhere near the foot of the cross for another ten years. Thankfully, there was no mountain high enough and no river wide enough to keep me from Christ forever.

It would not be accurate to say that Turkish culture is predominantly anti-Christian. Rather, it is simply against anything that might erode the amount of Islam necessary for Turkish identity. Judaism and Islamic sects, such as Alawism, are equally undesirable, though Christianity is at the top of the list of unwelcome religions. My maternal grandmother —may she rest in peace—was a calm, patient woman, which is why none of the grandchildren wanted to be around when she finally got angry. We could measure the level of her anger

by the epithets she used. If she accused any of us of being
"the seed of an Armenian", we knew that things were getting
serious. But when she started yelling that we were "seeds
of Jews", everyone under the legal drinking age scattered
around the house to avoid her wrath. I still not-so-fondly
remember my mother calling me "Greek-blooded" when I
was being stubborn. In short, one's lineage was brought into
question when one misbehaved. At least the insults did not
discriminate against any particular non-Muslim religion.

7

Troubled Adolescence

There I was, barely a teenager, with little parental supervision and even less moral guidance. Needless to say, things went downhill for a while. Since I had surrounded myself with similarly minded and misguided friends, as I drifted away from Islam, I started to embrace forbidden practices. First in line was alcohol.

In Turkey, many Muslims have a love-hate relationship with alcohol. Consumption of any alcoholic drink other than for medicinal purposes is strictly forbidden in Islam, as can be seen in Saudi Arabia and Iran. However, a variety of alcoholic drinks are available in every town in Turkey. Bars and clubs are not hard to find, and every major city has at least one street devoted to the patronage of nighttime drinkers. The legal age for drinking is eighteen, but it is not that hard for minors to gain access to alcohol. Many a time, I was able to enter a bar without an ID when I was barely fifteen. Rules were very malleable. So, after school until sunset, I spent my time drinking at a friend's house or at a deserted playground or along the train tracks or behind our school building. My friends and I mostly consumed wine or cherry-flavored vodka, and we tried not to get into trouble with anyone. Ours was the self-destructive kind of drinking that slowly made us feel more depressed and isolated. Almost all of us had trouble at home or at least had indifferent parents. What we could not find at home, we tried to find by diving into the bottle with our comrades.

Home was not a place I wanted to be. I could not wait until it was time to go to school in the morning, and I dreaded sunset, when I was supposed to return home. My mother either did not realize I was drinking on a regular basis or did not care what I was doing as long as I returned home in one piece without causing any nasty rumors in the neighborhood. The standards were not too high to meet, provided I was sneaky and cunning enough to appear to be an obedient daughter. All else was fair game.

Looking back, I feel deeply sorry for my mother. Her hard life had started well before she met my father, as she was the second of nine children born in a tiny village hugging the side of the Taurus Mountains. This remote village was hard to reach even when we visited my grandmother during the summer holidays, years after my mother's childhood. We would spend more than a month there every summer, chasing chickens, herding sheep, shoveling cow manure, and being harassed by geese.

The government did not want to waste money improving infrastructure because the area around the village was slated for a dam project and would soon be under water. It took decades for this project to begin, so all these people lived without indoor plumbing. One of my most unpleasant childhood memories involved using my grandmother's outhouse. I will not dwell on the experience. Needless to say, I am eternally grateful for the person who invented indoor plumbing.

In my grandmother's village, we also needed to haul pails of water from the only spigot in the area a few times a day.

Even though it was fun for the grandkids to be part of this daily ordeal, I am sure my grandmother would have deeply appreciated having one faucet at home. The harsh mountain winters of my mother's childhood were especially trying without a bathroom or running water.

Growing up, my brother and I frequently heard about the hardships of my mother's younger years, as my children will hear about the difficulties of my growing up in a house with only one bathroom and only three TV channels. When my brother and I complained about having to get up early for school, my mother would remind us that in wintertime she had to walk two miles in knee-deep snow to get to school. Mind you, we had to walk to school in freezing temperatures, too, without cancellations or two-hour delays. I cannot wait until I can use that against my own kids.

In addition to physical adversities, my grandfather did not believe that girls should be educated. My mother had to sneak out of the house or use my grandmother as a distraction in order to receive an elementary education. My grandmother was illiterate, and my oldest aunt did not continue schooling after the second grade. My mother, on the other hand, was determined to be the first female in the family to receive some formal education. She managed to complete fifth grade at the village school. Back then, there was a serious shortage of nurses, so nursing programs started at age twelve, right after fifth grade. My mother succeeded in getting into a nursing school and started to work as a nurse when she was a little older than fifteen.

My father and my mother met through one of my maternal uncles and got married in their early twenties. They married for love, but they were two completely different people. My father was an extrovert who liked joking, giving hugs, and pulling pranks on people. My mother, on the other hand, does not like jokes and being unnecessarily touched. On top of this, my father enjoyed being charming, especially to young women. Encouraged by the culture's tendency to favor the male sex, he sought what he could not find at home in other women.

As previously mentioned, when eventually my father decided to take an adulterous relationship to another level, and have a permanent mistress in the French fashion, my mother filed for divorce.

Back then, I did not know any other child whose parents were divorced. Thanks to all the bad stuff Turkey imported from the West, divorce is more common there now, but it was not when my mother decided to put an end to her marriage of fifteen years. Even though she was younger than forty, by the time my father left, she was already retired. Since my father refused to pay child support and to fulfill his legal responsibilities toward us with impunity, my mother single-handedly raised two kids, paid the mortgage, and endured those who looked down upon her. All these hardships and pressures, along with my teenage angst, made for a very disturbed mother-daughter relationship. Wanting to avoid my mom, I was tempted to sleep in the streets rather than go home, but thankfully I had a little more sense than that. Also, I had nowhere else to go.

We were poor because my mother's government pension was small. We weren't poor like the poor who have cable TV, internet service, and at least one car. I suppose the definition of "poor" depends on how the rest of the country lives, but many who are considered poor in the United States would be at least middle class in other countries. We were not destitute; we had a place to live and food to eat, but meat was a rare treat. My mother would buy a whole chicken, and we would make it last for about two weeks by putting small amounts of it in every dish for flavor and nutrition.

Red meat would be eaten only on rare occasions. The aforementioned holiday when Muslims sacrifice animals was the best time to eat meat, because much of the sacrificed animal is required to be distributed among those who cannot afford it themselves. We would get quite a bit of meat then, and we would make sausages and freeze as much as we could. The rest of the year we would often go vegetarian. But by no means were we nutritionally deprived, because fresh vegetables and fruits are much cheaper than processed food in Turkey. Our diet was also rich in beans and healthy grains. Even though we did not get to eat chips or chocolate regularly, and ice cream was a special treat we had every three months, we were sufficiently fed.

For us poverty meant that my brother and I wore our shoes until they fell apart, got fixed at the cobbler, and then fell apart again. It was the same for our jeans and coats: as long as the tears could be sewn or patched, we did not get new clothes. I don't really care about brand names or fancy clothes. I frequently visit thrift stores to buy secondhand clothing, because years of not having enough money to buy new clothes left me with the feeling that it is wasteful to spend a lot of money on clothing. But my teenage self begged to differ. I was very ashamed that we did not have enough money for me to dress like the other kids at my school.

When I passed the exam to go to a middle school for gifted children, this feeling of shame grew stronger. Although students were enrolled there according to their academic aptitude, most of them came from higher socio-economic classes. Even the "cool" friends I drank alcohol with could afford better clothing. I remember when Levi's 501 jeans became so popular that everyone owned a pair. But it was unthinkable for us to afford them then. When one of my cousins outgrew a pair of white Levi's jeans and gave them to me, I was happy beyond measure. I ended up tearing those jeans while trying to break into locked school grounds, but it was wonderful to have them while they lasted.

As my high school years approached, between drinking and being relatively poor, I started to feel more and more isolated from my peers. I still had a few friends who shared my views on Islam and had dysfunctional families, but my feeling of loneliness increased every year. I spent a significant amount of time reading. By the time I was in high school, I had read most of the classics, works of Nietzsche and Freud, and some by Kafka and Marx. At some point I even managed to read *The Lord of the Rings*, without seeing the story behind the elves and the hobbits. After the innocent years when I dreamed of living in one of Jules Verne's novels, I entered the suicidal undertones of Tolstoy and the homicidal tendencies of Engels.

During my last years of middle school, my cynicism grew like a weed, and my agnostic anti-Islamism turned into a concrete atheism. It was not a sudden change. After I learned what Marx, Kafka, Nietzsche, and some others thought about God, the final remnant of my humility, which whispered that humans were created beings, disappeared. In addition, I seemed to have found in science and mathematics the assurance that nature did not need a god and that there was nothing beyond the vast emptiness of the cosmos. As with any other religion, atheism has a moral code, whose main tenet is "Do whatever you like." Since I was already naturally prone to cynicism, it did not take me long to leave behind whatever moral constraints I once had. This loss did not immediately turn into a life of sin and debauchery, but I had no qualms about lying to my mother regularly or breaking the school rules whenever I felt like doing so. I was at the edge of the proverbial slippery slope. The already fragile relationship I had with my mother crumbled to pieces, and my heart became hardened toward her.

As my mother descended into depression and found solace in the therapy of crocheting day and night, I came home later and later and had less and less contact with her and my brother. I spent most of the day with my friends, either drinking or playing chess. When I had to spend time at home, I read.

My indifference to the world must have attracted the attention of some neighbors or my mom's friends, because one day my mother suggested that I see a psychiatrist. I was all too happy to accept her suggestion since doing so would get me out of the small town I hated and would give me access to pills that would numb my mind.

Some of my friends were already familiar with prescription drugs and had let me try a few. I had enjoyed the high I would get without the side effects of alcohol (my tolerance for alcohol was not very high). Thus started two years of trips to and from Ankara so that my teenage problems would be solved with a parent-approved pill bottle. During my first session, after seeing me for about ten minutes, the psychiatrist prescribed five drugs for me. Before I knew it, I was in a constant state of tipsiness and fog. When I slept, I did not dream, and when I was awake, it was as if I saw the world from behind a panel of frosted glass. My mind lost its sharpness. The longer I stayed on the drugs, the more indifferent I became to the rest of the world. Instead of removing the veil of my depression, the drugs pulled a curtain between me and everything else. I think therapy for my mother and me would have been more effective than numbing my mind, but it was easier for all involved, including the doctor, to push the trouble away rather than to confront it.

For a while, I enjoyed the high, but my dislike of isolation and my loss of mental sharpness slowly overpowered my desire to be slightly inebriated all the time. I loved reading and memorizing formulas for math class. As the drugs slowly took these simple joys away from me, I wanted to go back to my depressed self rather than completely lose myself. There was a guy in our chess circle who had an incredibly high IQ, but every time he went to see his psychiatrist, he would come back a zombie until his body adjusted to the drugs a little more. It was not hard to picture what kind of mind he would have had if he were not numbed and neutralized frequently. Even on his zombie-like days he could play chess with five of us at the same time and win effortlessly.

I did not want to be a zombie. Thus came my decision to quit the pills and leave the psychotropic-drug world once and for all. I did not talk to anyone or ask for permission to proceed. Neither my psychiatrist nor my mother knew what I wanted to do. In retrospect, it might have been a good idea to lower my dose of pills gradually, but instead I quit them cold turkey.

Watching all the little pills go down the toilet, hopefully never to be seen again, was wonderfully satisfying until about six hours later, when withdrawal symptoms began. For three days, I could not eat or have any restful sleep. When I dozed off from exhaustion, I would have weird black-and-white dreams and wake up cold and sweating. When my mother asked me why I had spent a whole day in my room without any food, I told her what I had done. She was neither upset nor encouraging, but indifferent, as usual. At least she left me alone. At the end of the three days, I felt much better. The fact that I was barely sixteen and otherwise physically in good shape probably hastened the cleansing process. But those three days of fits, sweat, shivering, and shaking continually reminded me to stay away from drugs. From then on, I would intoxicate my body only with alcohol and cigarettes.

In addition to drinking, I started smoking at the age of seventeen. These two habits were encouraged mostly by friends and some by my meager allowance. A few times, my friends and I experimented with pot, but thankfully it was an expensive and therefore rare pleasure for us. So, we stuck with getting drunk regularly and trying to break as many school rules as possible without getting caught. The punishment for drinking on school grounds, coming to class drunk, or possessing cigarettes was all the same: expulsion from the public school system. If a student was lucky, he might get one warning, but no one could count on that.

Thus went my high school years as an alienated teenager. I mostly damaged my body with self-indulgent, drunken, rebellious ways. All I wanted to do was to get out of my small town and move to a big city, where life would surely be much better. Little did I know that as long as I brought my sinful self with me, life would always be miserable.

8

Light in the Darkness

In Turkey the university entrance procedures are quite different from those in the United States. Instead of individually applying to one's desired college, every high school student takes a comprehensive exam at the end of his senior year. When my turn came to take the exam in 1998, the Turkish educational system combined the students' scores with their grade point averages to produce their final scores. All the scores from all the seniors in the country, about a million each year, were then ranked highest to lowest and placed in a percentile. Students would then apply to ten universities of their choice. The students in the higher percentiles were typically assigned to the more desirable schools.

I had managed to get into the top 1 percent, and I was accepted into the university in Istanbul, where classes are taught in French. The program required that I study for at least six years, because I needed two years of preparatory French classes.

I had never lived in such a large city, and moving to Istanbul, a city of ten million souls, was overwhelming. I needed help. By then my father was willing to rebuild our long-lost relationship, and my stepmother was willing to accept me into their lives. I moved into the small apartment they rented, and I commuted almost two hours each way to the university. My life changed dramatically in a matter of weeks.

Istanbul took my breath away. It is a beautiful city built around the Bosporus, a narrow strait that stretches from the Black Sea to the Sea of Marmara. The Roman emperor Constantine moved his capital to this location, renaming the city Constantinople. Slowly the city became a thriving center of culture and a crossroads for the rapidly growing Christian faith. Some even called it the "New Rome". The Byzantine capital became so important that Muhammad was believed to have promised heaven to the man who conquered it for Islam. By the time the city fell to the Ottoman Empire in 1453, the strength of the Byzantine Empire had significantly declined, its territories having been surrounded by Ottoman lands. The coveted city was conquered after an eight-week siege and the death of the last Roman emperor, Constantine XI. Sultan Mehmed II, "the Conqueror", made the city the capital of the Ottoman Empire and changed its fate forever. He renamed it Istanbul and turned Hagia Sophia, one of the largest and most magnificent churches in the world, into a mosque.

Thus began the transformation of Istanbul from a Christian hub to a center of Islamic culture. Despite the fact that the city remained in the hands of Ottoman Turks and had lost its former glory, its historical and strategic importance made the area desirable for many world powers at the end of World War I, when the Ottoman Empire was crumbling under the pressure of emerging nation-states. Having defeated the British, the French, and the Italians with the signing of the Treaty of Lausanne, which established most of the major boundaries of modern Turkey, the newly founded Turkish republic was able to hold on to one of the biggest conquests of the Ottomans.

There I was, in one of the most beautiful and populated cities in the world, and I felt completely lost and alone. Even though my father and stepmother welcomed me into their home, I remained a troubled eighteen-year-old who was not quite ready to be an adult. I had brought my baggage with me, and the glory of Istanbul could not rid me of it. In fact, my strained relationships with my father and my stepmother added to the load.

My father did not know how to relate to his not-so-little daughter, and he was a stranger to me. My stepmother was threatened by my presence for many reasons, one of which was that she was not much older than I. After a couple of months, my father's house made me miss my mother's cold but nonintrusive presence. Every encounter with my stepmother had become awkward, and we tried to avoid each other at all costs.

I should also note that I was completely financially dependent on my father. In Turkey, families take care of their children's needs until at least the end of college. It is almost unheard of for a college student to be responsible for his own expenses. Public universities are basically tuition-free, but room, board, and transportation are shouldered by parents. Not receiving any financial aid, I needed my father's support for the commute, meals, and books. At first, he was more than willing to make up for the lost years by being generous with me. But in about six months his eagerness diminished, and my dependency became a source of conflict between him and his wife.

Financial concerns plus the ever-increasing awkwardness eventually pushed my father and stepmother to ask me to move out. The eviction was a major problem for me, since I had neither money for rent nor friends I could room with. I felt once again betrayed and abandoned by the adults in my life, and my little faith in the concept of family burned to ashes, not to rise again for many years. The challenges Istanbul offered me became so overwhelming that by the end of the year I had no qualms about taking the dreaded university entrance exam again, so that I could transfer to a school in a less expensive city, far from either of my parents.

Ankara, the capital of Turkey, was my first choice, because I had friends there who were willing to share their apartment with me. I had also started to date an engineering student at a university there. I was restarting my life again at age of nineteen. By the time I left for Ankara, the relationship between my father and me was reduced to a thirty-second phone call every other month, and even that stopped after a while. I did not hear from him at all during my last few years of college. The situation with my mother was no different. She was happy that I was out of her hair. Yet she boasted that I was enrolled in a good university. The only familial tie that remained was with my brother, who was also trying to make ends meet while studying at a university in a different city. Once a month, we reminisced about our childhood and talked about how awful our parents were. Life in general was bleak, but at least in Ankara I had close friends and a supportive boyfriend.

The capital of Turkey is not nearly as illustrious as the capital of the former Ottoman Empire, but it was definitely an easier city to live in. Even though it is the second-largest metropolis in the country, with a population of more than four million, Ankara is less than half the size of Istanbul. Ankara is situated in ancient Galatia. Despite being a very old city, it was never as significant or populous as Istanbul. When the Ottomans were defeated after World War I, most of the territories in Anatolia were divided between the Allies, leaving the Turks the territory around Ankara. This old town became the center of the Turkish rebellion against both the Allies and the Ottoman sultanate. Mustafa

Kemal Atatürk, the founder of modern Turkey, established the headquarters of the resistance in Ankara, where he would be far from the influence of the Allies and the Ottoman throne. When the Turkish War of Independence successfully led to the founding of the Republic of Turkey, the new congress named Ankara the new capital, replacing Istanbul and leaving the days of the empire behind. Being the center of the country's political and military affairs, Ankara soon grew to be a major city, but unlike Istanbul its growth was more organized. In the end, despite not possessing the natural beauty or historicity of Istanbul, Ankara became a pleasant city. It hosted not only government agencies, but some of the best universities in the country. Eventually, it also became my new home.

Adjusting to life in the capital came much easier to me. The cost of living was lower, commuting was cheaper and less complicated, and I had the emotional support that I lacked in Istanbul. I worked a few jobs, but nothing was flexible enough for me both to study for the university entrance exam and to provide sufficient funds for my daily expenses. I lived in one of the residential areas of Ankara on a mighty hill. During the harsh, icy winters of central Anatolia, it was fun to watch cars go down that hill, completely at the mercy of gravity. Little did I know that this neighborhood would become the place where the seeds of the gospel would first be planted in my heart.

~

Yet another day of work and studies awaited me as I walked to the bus stop in the neighborhood on top of the hill. Cars and gas are very expensive in Turkey, and not many people know how to drive, but public transportation is easily accessible and relatively inexpensive. (I had no need to drive until I moved to a small mining town in Pennsylvania. Thanks to my husband's patient tutoring, I got my driver's license at the age of thirty-one.)

Unlike the Germans, we Turks are not a punctual people, and the big red bus to downtown was late, as usual. As I waited I glanced at various announcements in the sheltered bus stop. One of them informed me that a nearby American lady was looking for a college student to tutor her in Turkish. I sighed and thought that it would be wonderful not to have to commute to work. Also, tutoring would give me more time to study for my exam. But since I am prone to pessimism, I figured that she had probably already found somebody. Having arrived at this most logical conclusion, I went about my day without giving the matter another thought.

The day came and went. After long hours of filing cases at a lawyer's office, I was enjoying a quiet evening in my apartment with my roommates. Out of nowhere, the thought of the American lady came to mind. I didn't know why, but I was compelled to get her phone number. I felt sure that if I did not call the lady that very evening, I would suffer a sleepless night; some would call that an inspiration from the Holy Spirit. Off I went to the dark bus stop, where I wrote the number down in the dim light of my cell phone. Even though I have a strict rule about not calling anyone after 9:00 P.M., I found myself dialing the number. The woman who answered the phone spoke Turkish with a broken and clearly American accent. She said she had not hired anyone yet and would be happy to meet with me. We exchanged numbers and made an appointment. It was a good end to a long day.

Therese lived only a few streets down from my apartment. When the day of our appointment came, I slowly walked toward her building, not knowing what to expect from an American woman who lived in a decidedly Turkish part of the town occupied mostly by lower-middle-class families and students.

I was familiar with French and British cultures because of my previous studies, but my only encounter with American culture was the movies. Needless to say, my information was not very accurate. In most of the American movies that were shown on Turkish television, all the women were blonde and dressed as though they lived in Florida in August. Everyone drove expensive cars and lived in houses slightly smaller than mansions. *Knight Rider* and *Back to the Future* gave me the impression that talking cars and hover boards existed. Since moving to the States, I have been slightly disappointed that my house has only three bedrooms, my car refuses to converse with me, and my children's primitive skateboards have wheels. Where is the lifestyle Hollywood had dangled in front of me?

~

When I entered Therese's house, I was greeted by a graceful brunette in her thirties. Her apartment was decorated according to Turkish fashion and did not look out of place in the neighborhood. As far as I could see from the front door, the only thing one would not find in a typical Turkish household was the framed cross-stitch work, right across from the entrance. It appeared to be a verse from the New Testament:

> And there is salvation in no one else, for there is no other name under heaven given among men by which we must be saved. Acts 4:12

Since I was a militant atheist, it was one of the first things that attracted my attention. If Therese would hire me, I thought, the meaning and the meaninglessness of that verse would have to be addressed. I stuck a mental Post-it on the cross-stitch and proceeded to follow the American lady, trying to behave as politely as possible.

She welcomed me into her living room with the mandatory glass of tea that must accompany every conversation and business interaction in Turkey. It was a pleasant enough exchange about who I was, how much English I spoke, and what she expected from a tutor. She sounded self-confident and eager to learn. By then, my English was much better than that of many of my friends, even though French managed to occupy much of my brain's linguistic capacity. Because Therese was very new to the formidable Turkish language, she wanted someone who could explain things in English when needed.

Turkish is in the same language family as Korean and Japanese, and it sounds very different from English, or any other Germanic language. Also, the sentence structure and verb conjugation make Turkish very hard for most Westerners to master. Despite these difficulties, Therese was ready and enthusiastic to start our lessons. I was intrigued by this woman who did not shy away from undertaking such a challenge while mothering three children. We decided to meet again soon for our first session. I did not realize it then, but I was being drawn by a light that had begun to shine in the midst of the darkness.

9

Meetings with a Missionary

By the time I met Therese during the spring of 1999, I had succumbed to immorality and pessimism. In Ankara, I was blessed enough to have a loving boyfriend, Enver, who supported me in every way he could. But given my family background, I had lost faith in long-term relationships. I thought I loved him, but spending the rest of my life with him was unthinkable. I lived for the day. The future seemed not to hold any promises for me.

Living for the day also meant that I was free to do whatever I wanted. I had no qualms about premarital sex or drunkenness, both of which had become part of my life. Even though Enver shared my beliefs, or lack thereof, he had grown up in a more or less stable family, and he had a good relationship with his parents. He was therefore more open to staying together with me despite my insufferable pessimism. Thankfully, we were still too young to consider marriage. But this did not prevent us from trying to enjoy the benefits of a married life.

Of course, we were not ready for God to fulfill His promise to give life when we joined our bodies together. When we found out that I had gotten pregnant at the age of nineteen, we were both devastated. Teenage pregnancies are almost unheard of in Turkey because of the predominant shame culture and the lower rates of premarital sex. If an unmarried woman does become pregnant, she usually terminates the pregnancy secretly or in the privacy of the family.

Islam has a vague stance regarding abortion. Even though the Quran condemns the killing of persons, except for self-defense, national defense, and capital punishment, it does not mention abortion. Since the Quran does not explicitly forbid or permit abortion, Islamic theologians have varying opinions on it. The majority of theologians permit abortion up to day 40 of pregnancy, while others allow it until day 120, when the life force supposedly enters the body.

Yet more and more Muslims oppose all forms of abortion, citing a verse in the Quran: "Kill not your children for fear of want. We shall provide sustenance for them as well as for you. Verily the killing of them is a great sin (Surah 17:31)." It is also widely believed, however, that this verse refers to the killing of little children, especially girls, in the Arabian Peninsula in the days of Muhammad.

When the Quran outlines the development of the fetus in the womb, the description is physical, not spiritual:

> We created man from an essence of clay: then placed him, a living germ,

> In a secure enclosure. The germ We made a leech; and the leech a lump of flesh; and this We fashioned into bones, then clothed the bones with flesh;

> Then We developed it into another creation. (Surah Al-Mu'minoon 23:12-14)

During this physical development, the fetus supposedly receives the Divine Spirit, which is the person's life energy, but there is no consensus on when this life energy is infused and makes the fetus a person. Without a clear conviction that the human person is present from the moment of his conception, Islam has no clear teaching on whether or when abortion should be permitted. For instance, the morning-after pill in cases of rape is encouraged by Islamic scholars. Abortion when a mother's life is in danger is explicitly permitted. There have been cases of physical defects in which abortion was justified. The Hanafi school, which is the prominent school of Islamic thought in Turkey, teaches that Islam permits abortion up to four months of pregnancy. After this point, when the life force has been breathed into a fetus, abortion is akin to murder. The Hanbali school, prominent in Saudi Arabia and the United Arabic Emirates, prohibits abortion after day 40. Some Shiite groups permit no abortion at all.[1]

While I was growing up, the only time I heard about abortion was when one of our neighbors decided to have the baby "taken out" because she already had three children, one of whom was handicapped. Since 1982, abortion until the tenth week of pregnancy has been allowed in Turkey. Not until recently has abortion been considered a women's-rights concern. Mostly it was a nonissue, since Islam accepted early abortions, and their legality brought Turkey to the "level" of developed countries. Despite the civil legality and the religious permissiveness, I observed that Turkish women were reluctant to use abortion as birth control. Whatever the Islamic scholars say about the reception of the breath of life, women in their essence know that life begins

[1] Muhammad Rizvi, *Marriage and Morals in Islam* (Vancouver, B.C.: Vancouver Islamic Educational Foundation, 1990); Elsayed Kandil, "Abortion in Islam" (lecture given in Australia), Mission Islam, last accessed April 3, 2017, http://www.missionislam.com/health/abortion.htm; Yusuf Al-Qaradawi, *The Lawful and the Prohibited in Islam* (Plainfield, Ind.: American Trust Publications, 1994); Khalid Farooq Akbar, "Family Planning and Islam: A Review", *Hamdard Islamicus* 17, no. 3 (1974).

at conception. Despite the reluctance of Turkish women to terminate their pregnancies, the abortion rate is still high in Turkey.

For me, having the baby was not something I considered even for a moment. First of all, I did not believe that it was a baby. It was just a cluster of tissues that posed a threat to my current lifestyle and especially to my future. Enver and I did not even have a discussion about it. As soon as the urine test showed positive, we made an appointment with a gynecologist who performs abortions. I did not have the money, but my boyfriend could easily pay the eighty dollars needed to get rid of our "problem".

We showed up at the respectable-looking doctor's office in a nice neighborhood of the city. As far as we knew, he was a good doctor who also delivered babies and specialized in ovarian cancer. On the side, he happened to help women by getting rid of their clusters of tissue that could one day become babies. As I looked around, I felt uncomfortable to be in a place where life and death occupied the same room with such ease. Part of me did not want to be there, but a bigger and more selfish side of me argued that my problem needed to be solved.

The doctor asked me questions about my medical history and inquired if I was allergic to anything. He sounded professional and concise. Not once did he question my age or show any curiosity about our marital status. His desire to steer clear of such inquiries made me believe that he was used to seeing couples like us, in addition to seeing parents who visit his office happily for prenatal checkups. I wanted to leave the place as soon as possible. He assured me that the "procedure" would be over in an hour and that I could leave as soon as the dizziness from the anesthesia passed. A nurse directed me to a clean, well-kept room, fully equipped with the tools of this doctor's trade. The operation table awaited me. Without a second thought I settled on it.

Shortly after, the anesthesiologist injected me with a drug that put me to sleep for the hour that the doctor needed to get me back to my problem-free life. When I woke up, it was all done. I had successfully killed my first baby without much thought or many questions, and for very little money.

After that day, my relationship with Enver went downhill. Even though he had by no means forced me to have an abortion, I slowly drifted away from him. My reluctance to commit to someone for any length of time, my lack of trust, and my unwillingness to look beyond the present all contributed to our downfall. The chemistry of falling in love never turned into the settled and mature love of a life-long relationship. On top of all these factors, the abortion added another obstacle for us to work through. Having participated in something inherently evil, we had severed what connection we had in our sinful relationship. I broke up with him less than a year later.

It was around the fateful time of my abortion that I started working for Therese. My life was full of self-indulgence, but I had not the eyes to see it. I was also arrogant, for I thought I had long ago figured out the secrets of the universe and of my own being by reading about the cosmos and the theory of evolution.

Little did I know that Therese's carefully embroidered verse would change my life forever:

> And there is salvation in no one else, for there is no other name under heaven given among men by which we must be saved. Acts 4:12

~

When Therese opened the door for the first of countless tutoring sessions, she probably did not know what to expect from this self-satisfied teenager. She led me to the room where we had our first interview, where we sat on blue corduroy chairs around the dining room table. She had put a delicate-looking crochet cloth on the table and had piled her materials for language learning on top. I could tell that she was determined to crack the code.

She was ready as a student, but I was less than adequate as a tutor. I had tutored children in mathematics when I was in high school, but that was the extent of my teaching experience. She had taken a leap of faith to pick me, and I wanted to help her as much as I could. Thankfully, my many years of preparing for the university entrance exam and the hours of learning the mercilessly irregular English language had made me an expert in both Turkish and English grammar. I have a hard time holding my tongue when I hear others' grammar mistakes.

Settled around the table, sipping our third glass of Turkish tea, Therese and I began talking about matters of the soul. For my part, I was eager to help this poor woman whose mind had been poisoned with religion and the constraints of society. On the other hand, Therese was eager to share with a lost teenager the faith and the miracle that had changed her life. After all, that was the reason she had left everything and everyone she knew and moved to a Muslim country with her husband and three young children. She would not dare tell me that she was a missionary, since the word has a very negative connotation in my country. It is called the M-word, and people who communicate with Christian missionaries in Turkey are strongly discouraged from using it in their correspondence. Instead the term "worker" is employed.

The reasons for this irrational fear of missionaries are manifold. An anti-Christian attitude is a big part of the national identity, so anyone or anything that promotes Christianity is automatically suspicious. Also, as is the case in many Muslim countries, the Crusades have often been distorted in order to convince Muslims that Christians want to destroy them and obliterate Islam. In middle school and high school textbooks, the Crusades are presented as the Catholic Church's efforts to dominate the Orthodox Church and Islam in the Holy Land. The Crusades were wars of aggression, not defense. It was the Christians who wanted to plunder the lands and the riches of the Muslim world. All the Turks did was defend what was rightfully theirs. (No longer a naïve young student, I know that reality is slightly different from what was written in my Turkish history books.)

Having thus heard many times a skewed version of history, many Turks are prejudiced against Christianity. They therefore see missionaries in Turkey as agents of foreign powers who want to undermine the Turkish government and way of life. Missionaries are perceived not as those who want to share their faith and lead others to salvation, but as sinister people who would do anything to expand their sphere of influence. Unlike Muslims, it is argued, Christians offer material gains, education, or promises of travel to achieve their ends. Lying and deception are the tools of their trade. Needless to say, in the long history of missionary efforts, Christians have made some mistakes that they should not duplicate. And these are combined with imaginary misdeeds to create a formidable barrier between Christian missionaries and Turks.

Even though everyone who takes his religion seriously is naturally a missionary, a Christian who leaves everything behind and moves to a hostile mission field is exercising his calling on a heroic level. I admire those who choose this path of life so that the Word of God can reach more people. Unfortunately, missionary zeal is lacking in the Catholic Church. Our Protestant brethren shoulder most of the burden of evangelization, and a burden it is. Living in lands like Turkey that are extremely resistant to the gospel is very difficult. I pray that Catholic laity will be inspired to join the missionary clergy who serve in other countries and lighten their burden.

Since I was an atheist, and I had no qualms about spreading my own "faith", I was the one who brought up the subject of religion with Therese. The Lord knew that I needed a woman who was as intellectual and stubborn as I was. We didn't have the tentative and gentle relationship of two women. If someone had observed one of our heated discussions, he would have thought of two grouchy rams fighting with their horns, neither of them willing to yield. In many ways, these discussions were refreshing. Over the years, I had surrounded myself with people who thought and believed what I thought and believed. We enjoyed making fun of Islam and Muslims and reading about evolution and quantum physics. There's nothing like being smarter than everyone else. Thankfully God knows me better than I know myself, and He sent someone who would not hesitate to put me in my place.

Therese had studied at a prominent American university, and she loved reading. She would read about anything and everything (although she never developed a taste for science fiction, which remains a fault of hers). She was knowledgeable in many subjects, especially Islam and atheism. In addition to being almost always ready to deflect my attacks with accurate information, she was able to use the Socratic method so cleverly that I myself would question the way I thought. Our friendship was a match made in heaven.

Over the course of three years of tutoring sessions, we

talked about many topics, mostly related to God and sometimes politics or economics. I still had a strong attachment to communist ideals, since I believed that the utopia promised in communism was attainable and was the promise of heaven on earth. This hope was especially important because I believed that there was no heaven, no life after death. The strict structure of socialism was only a stepping stone to the promised land of communism, and one should be willing to endure some hardship for a greater reward. My adherence to communism revealed my belief that a perfect man-made political and economic structure was possible.

The major difference of opinion between Therese and me boiled down to what we believed in regard to human nature. I believed that people are inherently good and that there is no such thing as sin. People act the way they do because of the way they were raised or because of society's unjust treatment and expectations of them. If people were freed from unnecessary rules and laws, we would all live in peace and harmony, I thought. All the expectations of living together as social beings and the supposed wisdom of generations put undue pressure on otherwise good people and made them go astray. Add income inequality and poverty, and there was the recipe for crime and war. The only solution was to remove all this baggage. It would take some time and effort to eliminate all traces of organized religion, government, and capitalism, but I was hopeful.

Such were the concepts in my arrogant head, but I was far from doing anything about putting them into practice, about bringing about a new world. My days of going to socialist party meetings and attending demonstrations were behind me. All I cared about was getting into the university. I desired and continued to live my selfish and pretentious life. Somebody else would have to start the revolution.

Christianity, on the other hand, is based on the fact that

people are flawed and weak—sinful, in other words. If they were not, there would be no need for Christ's sacrifice. The Crucifixion of Jesus would be a tragic death, a meaningless injustice, nothing more. According to Therese's Christian faith, we sinners need a savior. But like many people, I was unconvinced of my need for divine assistance. I was like a man at the bottom of a well who had no idea he needed a rope thrown down to him.

As if my ignorance and arrogance were not enough, I was also sure that somebody else was responsible for my miserable life. A logical consequence of denying the existence of one's sins is blaming others for one's unhappiness. I was the way I was because my parents got divorced. That man robbed a bank because wealth is unevenly distributed. People commit rape because society puts too much pressure on individuals to control their sexual desires. Murder too, I thought, was caused by the buildup of pressure on individuals who were not given the tools they needed to make it in society. To this day, I have not met a murderer. My husband, on the other hand, worked on death row at a state prison. Society, he says, doesn't have much to do with the way men condemned to die turned out.

My atheism relieved me of the burdens of conscience. My roommate shoplifted regularly and shared her loot with us. Even though I was too much of a chicken to steal, I was more than happy to partake of ill-gotten goods. My roommate and I believed that the rich man had acquired this wealth unjustly by cheating others, so why should we not take it from him? Premarital sex was not an issue at all, because sex was a natural need and suppression of sexual desires leads to aggression and violence. Besides, marriage was nothing more than a social construct to enslave individuals. Abortion was not murder because a fetus is a bunch of cells and nothing more.

So on one hand, I was full of condemnation toward the ills of my family and my society. But on the other hand, I was full of laxity toward myself. My attitude was like that described by G. K. Chesterton in his book *What's Wrong with the World*:

> I maintain, therefore, that the common sociological method is quite useless: that of first dissecting abject poverty or cataloguing prostitution. We all dislike abject poverty; but it might be another business if we began to discuss independent and dignified poverty. We all disapprove of prostitution; but we do not all approve of purity. The only way to discuss the social evil is to get at once to the social ideal. We can all see the national madness; but what is national sanity? I have called this book "What Is Wrong with the World?" and the upshot of the title can be easily and clearly stated. What is wrong is that we do not ask what is right.[2]

That was exactly my problem: I never asked what was right. All I wanted to do was to point out what I thought needed to be fixed in my family, my society, my former religion. I never looked at what might need to be fixed in myself. That is, I never took a good look until I met Therese.

[2] G. K. Chesterton, *What's Wrong with the World* (San Francisco: Ignatius Press, 1994), p. 17.

10

Searching for God

As I tutored Therese, my quest for the truth intensified. Mercifully, she was willing to be my compass during that stormy odyssey.

We disagreed about almost everything, and her consistency and logic became more and more annoying. Often after our sessions I would go home and do some research so that I could disprove her points next time. I just hated being wrong or unable to produce a counterargument. There were many atheists who were much smarter and wiser than I. Surely they had come up with some foolproof reasons for being an atheist.

I needed intellectual backup because I had not thought my way to atheism. Rather, I had slid into it—by lacking any reason to adhere to a religion and living as though it did not matter. Therefore, when confronted with reasonable questions about my chosen faith, I did not have any answers, other than that I did not have any evidence for God's existence.

Over the years, I had come to worship modern, atheistic science, which claims that there is no proof for an all-powerful, benevolent God and that the universe is only matter. Everything in it could be explained with the scientific method, I thought. There was no room for God in the tightly woven tapestry of material causes and effects. Not until I met Therese, and began searching for answers to her questions, did I begin to discover the weaknesses in my view of the world.

I came to see that my basic problem was a matter of perception. Science has demonstrated that everything in the universe is finely tuned, particularly for life to be sustained on earth. Rather than being the grounds for atheism, could not the discoveries of science point toward a Creator, who values life and therefore designed the conditions for its existence?

Then there is the matter of beauty. I had always admired the beauty of nature. Watching a glorious sunset, glimpsing a full moon through the trees of a pine forest, walking in cool, quiet woods on an autumn afternoon—such experiences occupied special places in my heart. For the consistent materialist, however, the emotions stirred by these experiences are nothing more than the chemical reactions of the body to sensory stimuli, just as the luscious colors of the sunset are merely the result of the sun's rays penetrating the atmosphere at different angles.

But looked at another way, could not all this beauty be appreciated as the work of a divine Artist? Could not the fact that beauty brings us joy be attributed to God's generosity toward us? Knowing scientifically the physical causes of the colors of the sunset does not eliminate the possibility of God. Knowing the chemical processes at work in our bodies does not preclude the realization that we are wonderfully made to enjoy the abundant gifts that God pours into our laps.

When I look at my newborn, I am amazed at how perfectly he is formed despite the fact that thousands of things could have gone wrong when he was developing in the womb. The old me would have simply admired how perfectly evolution works. The new me is amazed at the miracle a child is.

This change in perception did not come to me overnight; it was a long process. Day in and day out, Therese and I talked about God and Christ and the necessity of His sacrifice. I was not ready to hear about Christ at first, but it became harder and harder to insist that there was no God. Slowly, the realization dawned that evolution and God, science and religion, were not mutually exclusive. Before, I had brushed off religious scientists as romantics. After a while, I could see that maybe their universe was bigger than mine. If there was a God, He would be the one who created a universe whose laws were consistent so that a scientist on earth could expect the speed of light to be the same here and also in another galaxy with different stars. Similarly, the omnipotent Creator could use evolution to bring about different forms of life or make the sun the center of our solar system so that men did not think that they were the center of the universe. If I could stop looking only at the building, I could open my mind to the possibility of an Architect.

Another topic of discussion that helped me to understand God was childrearing. Therese and her husband, Francis, had the first functional family I could witness up close. Since my own family had fallen apart almost a decade before, I was very curious about their family dynamics. As far as I had observed, even the couples I knew who stayed together did not have the love and the connection that Therese and Francis shared. Therese always said that Francis was a blessing, that he was God's greatest gift to her. This was a new concept for me, because in Turkey women always mention their children as God's greatest gift. The relationship between Francis and Therese was very different from anything I had ever seen or heard.

Therese and Francis had three children, ages five, three, and six months, close in age to my own children at the time of this writing. I know even better now than I did then what a challenge it is to mother children during their younger years. Therese was both strict and loving, which was a paradox to me, since in my experience a parent was either one or the other. My mother did not punish to discipline me but to satisfy her anger. My father was not involved in our disciplining and thus seemed, from a childish perspective, the kinder of the two. In short, I had never experienced being disciplined by a loving parent. Getting to know Therese's children, however, I could see the positive results of growing up in a loving, caring home that had boundaries.

As a parent, I know that children thrive when they have guidance as they explore the world. They feel safe and secure. That was how Therese's children felt, as evidenced by the way they behaved. Of course, they acted up from time to time—threw their toys, refused to share, and so on— thank you, human nature! But Therese was patient and attentive when her children needed correction. She reproved them firmly but kindly. I am sure there were days when she wanted to lock herself in a closet and eat a giant chocolate bar, but her faith strengthened her to persevere in doing what she knew was best for her children even when it was difficult. I did not immediately make the connection between their being Christians and having a much happier home than mine. Slowly Christ's light on this loving family became clear to me.

At the end of the first year of our challenging friendship, I had grown to like and to care for Therese and her family. She continued to drive me crazy, but it was becoming harder and harder for me to find rebuttals for her arguments. Years after our friendship matured, Therese told me that during those early days she sometimes feared that she had gone too far. Many times she did not expect me to return, but she prayed for me regardless. I never once considered not returning. It is true that we had many heated and at times annoying arguments, but she was the only one I knew who held a glimmer of light, a sliver of hope, in the darkness. If nothing else, curiosity about where that light came from brought me back time after time. I was not sure what I believed anymore, and I wanted the freedom that the truth might bring. But that prospect was unnerving, as Dumbledore says to Harry Potter: "The truth is a beautiful and terrible thing, and should therefore be treated with great caution."

~

As my inner struggles continued, life went on. After having retaken the university entrance exam, I managed to enter Middle East Technical University (METU). It is Turkey's top school and the one I was striving for. My major was international relations. By the time classes started, I had broken up with Enver and started dating Alp, a student in an engineering department of the same university. He was a gentle, sensitive man who genuinely cared for me. He was also much less cynical than I was, especially when it came to God and religion. Agnosticism rather than outright atheism was more Alp's style.

Not long after we started dating, we decided to live together, and I moved into the apartment he shared with his mother and his sister near the university campus, not far from where Therese lived. Alp and I shared a room, and his mother and his sister occupied the other two bedrooms. They did not care that we were enjoying spousal privileges without a spousal commitment.

Therese came to visit us and to see my latest living accommodations. After more than a decade, I still vividly remember the disappointment I saw in her face when she saw the bed I shared with Alp. Despite her disapproval, she was gracious enough to hold her tongue, because she knew that I was not ready to respond to the truth.

The apartment where Alp and I lived with his family was small. Even though Alp's parents were not divorced, they did not live together, for they could not tolerate each other's company. His father lived in Izmir, ancient Smyrna. Alp's mother was a kind, gentle, and selfless woman. She always had a smile on her face and was ever ready to be helpful, but she was broken. She could not escape the insecurities of being an unloved woman in Turkey. Not having anything other than her children to anchor her to the world, she was always depressed under the never-ending smile. Alp's sister was also insecure, in addition to being an introvert. Being perpetually overwhelmed by the company of others, I related to her desire for solitude. Looking back, however, I can see that my retreat from people was more an escape than an effort to recharge. Alp's sister was a lawyer at the beginning of her career, but she did not seem satisfied with her job or her place in life. Among these unhappy souls, Alp and I fit right in.

Having grown up in a broken family in addition to being naturally sensitive, Alp developed a talent for music, which provided him with a needed escape. His favorite style, however, was heavy metal. He would listen to hard rock for hours, and he tried to get me to enjoy it as well. Not a chance. To this day, I cannot stand loud music and people screaming instead of singing intelligible lyrics.

Despite his long hair and his choice of music, Alp had a sensitive heart. He always spoke softly—he hardly ever raised his voice—and he was always kind to everybody. I felt safe and loved around him, and his devotion to me was obvious to everyone who knew us. We seemed to be a perfectly happy and well-matched couple, but in reality my inner life had started to change.

During this time of slow heart change I got pregnant again. How silly it was for us to think that something called the birth control pill would let us have consequence-free sex. I was again faced with the decision to make the trip to the sterile doctor's office, but this time with another man. The decision was not as easy as it was before, but I was convinced that there was no way for us to have a baby while we both were in college. Although we were in better financial shape than two years before, neither of us was selfless enough to welcome our own child into our lives. We hid behind the trite arguments and took the bus to the doctor's office. Everything was the same as before. No questions asked, the fees paid, anesthetics administered, baby killed, and problem solved. This time, however, nightmares and cold sweats plagued me for more than a week. Dark imaginings of bloody beaches and distant cries haunted my nights, making me afraid of going to sleep. The light of the Holy Spirit was seeping in, and I did not like what He revealed. Still, years of practice helped me to quiet my conscience.

Therese was the first pro-life person I had ever known. Her conviction about life beginning at conception was so strong and inspiring that even though I did not agree with her, I was envious of the confidence she exuded. Her unyielding position on abortion touched me deeply. Whole-heartedly I wanted her to be wrong. I wanted to dismiss her as an antifeminist, religious nut job, but the science that was my god proved that the cluster of tissues removed by an abortion has a heartbeat. An ultrasound image of a human embryo does not depict an amorphous glob, but the distinct shape and the developing organs of a human person. As Therese and I discussed abortion, I argued that women needed to have access to birth control methods, including abortion, in order to free themselves from the tyranny of men, although I knew that abortion victimized and scarred women. Even I, as a pragmatic, selfish atheist, experienced sorrow over my abortions. For a long time, I managed to silence my sadness and defend my actions. Eventually, however, largely due to Therese, I became pro-life well before I started to believe in God.

Not long after I moved in with Alp, I started to read more about the rational basis for belief in God. As I did so, I paid increasing attention to what Therese was saying. Outwardly I was still my cynical and sarcastic self, but inwardly I started to take her seriously, to imagine the possibility of an after-life, for example. Little by little, my faith in atheism was crumbling. Odd as it sounds, atheism is also a faith: It is the belief that God does not exist, a declaration that cannot be proved. It requires constant effort to deny the existence of God, because He has created us with a desire to know Him and to love Him. Resisting this desire got harder and harder for me. Once I began giving in a little to my inborn spiritual nature, my journey toward God picked up the pace.

Even after discovering within myself the potential to believe in God, I still did not want to be a follower. The problem of pain was a big stumbling block for me. As I mentioned before, I believed that people are inherently good.

By removing the sinful nature of man from the equation, I naturally concluded that God, if He exists, is the ultimate perpetrator of evil in the world. Being omniscient and omnipotent, God has the knowledge and the means to prevent all the pain in the world, but He chooses not to. Despite my claim of being intelligent and knowledgeable, I could not grasp the concept of free will and its logical consequences. As far as I could tell, God must be selfish and capricious, and I would rather turn my back on Him than worship Him.

Thankfully, the Holy Spirit is more stubborn than I am.

11

Grand Inquisitor

During this time of spiritual struggle, I was nearing the end of my freshman year at METU. The instructional language at METU is English. Since English is a foreign language for most METU students, the university brought in American professors to expose the students to authentic pronunciation and more relevant vocabulary. My class was lucky to have a Fulbright scholar teach our advanced English course.

To be honest, trying to read the *Economist* as non-native English speakers was a painful endeavor. We not only needed to understand and summarize the articles, but we also had to learn some excruciating vocabulary that the English language produced just to torture foreign students. Words such as "ubiquitous", "idiosyncratic", and "auspicious" gave some of us ulcers as we tried to pronounce and spell them. To improve our comprehension, we watched CNN and read English literature and English translations of European classics.

One of the assignments given by our Buddhist American professor shattered my view of human nature. When he distributed copies of a chapter from Fyodor Dostoyevsky's *The Brothers Karamazov*, we all sighed and complained, in the manner of college students everywhere, especially because it was an older English translation of the work. It was going to be a long night with our beloved dictionaries.

I had already read many of Dostoyevsky's works when I was a teenager, but thankfully they had all been translated into Turkish and were therefore relatively pain-free to read. Dostoyevsky was a Russian novelist who lived in the nineteenth century and authored many acclaimed works, such as *Crime and Punishment*, *The Idiot*, *Demons*, and *Notes from Underground*. *The Brothers Karamazov* is considered his greatest novel. Dostoyevsky was raised in an Orthodox family and was exposed to the Gospels from an early age. He grew up making regular visits to monasteries with his family, and eventually he became devoted to the Orthodox faith; he had a strong prayer life. It is said that many people in the Soviet Union kept their faith because of his writings, since all other religiously inspired literature was destroyed by the communist regime.

The assignment that made my class groan was Dostoyevsky's most famous chapter, "The Grand Inquisitor". Little did I suspect that in a matter of hours this piece would turn my life upside down. The chapter is a parable told by Ivan, the brother who questions the existence of a benevolent Supreme Being. Alyosha, the brother who is a novice monk, is Ivan's audience, because the cynical older brother wants to make his younger sibling question his faith. It is a rather anti-Catholic parable, but God works in mysterious ways.

The tale starts with Christ's coming to Seville during the Spanish Inquisition. It is not the Second Coming; the Son of God is just stopping by for a visit.

He performs miracles similar to the ones in the Gospels. He walks about the crowd, cures a blind man, and raises a little girl from the dead. Everyone recognizes Him as He moves quietly with a gentle smile on His face. The crowd thickens around their Savior at the bottom of the stairs of the cathedral, where He has raised the little girl not long ago. As it happens, the grand inquisitor, the chief of the Spanish Inquisition, passes by the cathedral as the crowd kneels before Christ. The inquisitor is an old man, dressed in a simple monk's habit. The old cardinal witnesses all the miracles and the crowd's adoration. Then he motions to the guards to arrest Christ. The crowd cowers before the prelate, and not one person voices a protest, even after having seen Christ's miracles. The guards take the Son of God to a dark prison cell.

The inquisitor visits Christ in the prison and tells Him that the Church no longer needs Him. He explains that Christ's return would interfere with the Church's mission and frames his reasons around Satan's temptations of Christ in the desert. He tells Christ that man was not worthy of the freedom God bestowed upon him at Creation. Men are too weak to remain faithful to Him. Instead of freedom, Christ should have given man security. Since His departure, the inquisitor explains the Church has been trying to eradicate the freedom the Son of God provided and perfected centuries ago upon the cross. The Church has been doing this to make the faithful truly happy, thus correcting God's error in judgment.

The first temptation Satan offered Christ was food. Having fasted for forty days, Christ was challenged by Satan to turn stones into bread, if He indeed was the Son of God. Jesus answered: "Man shall not live by bread alone, but by every word that proceeds from the mouth of God" (Mt 4:4).

The inquisitor says that, unlike Christ, most men are not strong enough to live by the word of God. Jesus should have grabbed the power to turn stones into bread and thus freed mankind from hunger, instead of giving him freedom.

In the second temptation, Satan took Christ to a high

point in Jerusalem and told Him to prove that He was the Messiah by throwing Himself off the edge. If He was truly the Son of God, Satan said, the angels would lift Him up. Christ answered: "You shall not tempt the Lord your God" (Mt 4:7).

The inquisitor argues that man needs a supernatural being to worship in order to be content. Thus, Christ should have answered this need by giving men such awesome signs and wonders that they would be forced to believe in Him. Instead, Christ shrouded His power in subtlety and mystery and gave foolish men the choice to follow their hearts.

The third temptation of Christ was about power over mankind. Satan took Jesus to a high mountain, showed Him all the kingdoms of the earth, and offered them to Christ if He would bow down and worship him. But Jesus replied: "Begone, Satan! for it is written, 'You shall worship the Lord your God and him only shall you serve'" (Mt 4:10).

The inquisitor tells his Lord that He should have grabbed the authority Satan offered Him and established the universal state. Men always crave order, he says, and for this they will accept rule by tyrants. By refusing to pick up Caesar's purple cloak, Jesus forced the Church to pick up Caesar's sword and to bring order through the use of force.

"In truth, Thou didst Thyself lay the foundation for the destruction of Thy kingdom, and no one is more to blame for it. Yet what was offered Thee? There are three powers, three powers alone, able to conquer and to hold captive forever the conscience of these impotent rebels for their happiness—those forces are miracle, mystery and authority."[1]

The inquisitor concludes his monologue by saying that the Church had to do what God Himself had failed to ac-

[1] Fyodor Dostoyevsky, *The Brothers Karamazov* (New York: North Point Press, 1990), p. 260.

complish: take away freedom in exchange for bread and security. This has to be done, not because the Church is evil or worships Satan, but because this is the only way to establish order for mankind.

After the grand inquisitor finishes giving his verdict, Christ says not a word in response. Rather, He walks up to the old man and kisses him gently on the lips. The cardinal sets the Prisoner free, telling Him never to return.

After hearing Ivan's tale, instead of doubting his chosen way of life, Alyosha leans over and kisses his brother on the lips, just as Christ had kissed the inquisitor.

The parable is a reflection of Ivan's inner struggle with the Deity. Even though the cynical brother does not necessarily deny God's existence, he rejects Him because His gift of freedom allows too much suffering in the world. He vividly describes to Alyosha some harrowing examples of human cruelty in order to justify his refusal to kneel before a King who would allow such evil when He has the power to end it.

I deeply sympathized with Ivan. How easy it would have been to side with darkness and despair after having read this rather difficult text. But there I was, in the middle of the night, after many cups of tea and agonizing hours spent deciphering the words of Dostoyevsky, stunned to silence with an unfamiliar ache in my stomach. Ivan's intention was to push Alyosha away from his devotion to a God who would not eradicate suffering with a snap of His fingers. But Ivan failed to change the heart of the young novice, who grasped God's love for mankind, even in the midst of evil.

Alyosha's purity and steadfastness drew me to him. A light came on at some point during the long night, and I understood what it means to be truly free. There is both beauty and misery hidden within freedom. It is not that God lets us down; it is that we let Him down. The suffering in the world is not God's doing; it is ours. We inflict suffering upon each other, upon ourselves. There is much hunger in the world, not because the earth is insufficient to feed us all, but because some take too much or because governments abuse their power. Ruling classes are made of people, sinful people. There are wars and conflicts because people crave power and are willing to use their strength to take away the freedoms and even lives of others.

It was the first time I had comprehended what it means to live in a fallen world. I saw that human nature is not inherently good; it is inherently flawed. Left to our own devices, we all succumb to our evil inclinations and sin against God and others. I realized that it is not society's fault that there are rapists and murderers. Nor are religions to blame for war. All that is wrong with the world is what is wrong with us—since the fall of Adam and Eve, our intellects have been darkened and our wills weakened.

This moment of realization was also the first time I truly saw myself in the mirror. I was not an exception to the rest of the human race. I was not a victim. As with everyone else, my sins were countless. I had hurt others, just as others hurt me. I blamed my parents for many things that went wrong in my life, but I had made a myriad of bad decisions myself. My father's selfishness had scarred my whole family, but my selfishness had given pain to wonderful men and killed my own babies. My mother's pride had prevented her from being a good mother, but my own pride had made me a cold, unreachable daughter, sister, and friend. There were greed, lust, and gluttony in my life, and I was as helpless as everyone else to overcome these vices on my own.

Reading Dostoyevsky's century-old words changed my life forever. When God gave us free will, He knew what our freedom would cost Him. In His infinite love and mercy, rather than enslaving us, the Son of God preferred to die to save us from the pit we dug for ourselves.

As I rose from my desk that was covered in books, papers, and coffee stains, I knew that Therese was right. Even though I hated to accept that I was wrong, I could not help but sense relief. I felt like a mathematician who had solved the equation that had taunted him for ages. I had found the solution. More accurately, the solution had found me. Now all I had to do was to acknowledge it. But it would be another six months before I could finally, externally acknowledge what had internally taken place. Pride was a mighty opponent, as Archbishop Fulton Sheen so wisely said: "Pride is an admission of weakness; it secretly fears all competition and dreads all rivals."[2]

[2] Fulton Sheen, *Life Is Worth Living* (San Francisco: Ignatius Press, 1999), p. 44.

12

Burying My Head in the Sand

I read "The Grand Inquisitor" at the end of my freshman year. As I finished my finals, life threw so many curve balls at me that I did not immediately act on the profound realization of that sleepless night. First of all, I needed to move into a dorm. Alp had accepted a position in a university seven hours away, and we could no longer live together. We would be able to see each other every other weekend, instead of every day. This change was drastic for me, as Alp had become a pillar I leaned against. Secondly, Therese and her family were going back to the United States for a year, leaving me without a job. Because I had come to depend financially on our tutoring sessions, losing that income was another significant blow for me. Worries of the flesh took over.

A little before my encounter with Ivan and Alyosha, Alp and I had decided to get engaged so that we could tell our families that there was some form of commitment between us. Neither of us really believed in marriage. There was no official proposal, no flowers, no ring, and no pictures. It was a cold decision based on a detached conclusion that we needed to please our parents. Marriage was not sacred or special to us. On the contrary, it was yet another mechanism for society to control us. Despite all my criticisms of marriage, our relationship became much more serious once the terms "engagement" and "fiancé" started to be thrown around. The weight of our new situation was heavier than I had expected.

Another reason my lesson from Dostoyevsky resided behind locked doors in my mind was that I now understood what it meant to accept Christ's sacrifice. Turkish Christians are persecuted, sometimes outwardly, more often subtly. Christian converts in Turkey are rejected by their family and friends. In some cases their parents lock them up at home in an attempt to cut them off from outside influences. The reaction of a convert's family depends on where they lived and how religious they are. In civil society, conversion to Christianity means that one has become a traitor to the Turkish state. Treason and espionage are often mentioned when someone talks about Christianity on a regular basis. On top of all this, the punishment for apostasy in Islam is death, although when I was undergoing conversion, I had not heard of anyone in Turkey being executed by Islamists for becoming a Christian.

Since 2005, however, there have been executions of apostates and infidels. In 2006, the Catholic priest Andrea Santoro was murdered by a teenager as he knelt in prayer before the altar. In 2007, Armenian journalist Hrant Dink was murdered for "insulting Turkishness", and Necati Aydin, Ugur Yuksel, and Tilmann Geske had their throats slit at a Christian bookstore. None of these atrocities had happened yet at the time of my struggle with Christianity, but I knew about the darkness and the hardness of Turkish hearts when it came to Christ.

I knew that if I were to choose to follow Christ, I would become a stranger in my own land, like many before me.

In addition, it would be practically impossible for me to get a government job if I converted to Christianity. I was studying at one of the best universities in the country, and most of my friends would go on to get respectable positions in various government ministries. Those doors would be closed to me, because the Turkish government would no longer trust me on account of my new religious affiliation. I did not want to give up all the comforts that a life without Christ could offer.

Contemplating what all my friends would think of me if I became Christian weighed on me. I was surrounded by people who were either atheist or agnostic. I had only one practicing Muslim friend. He was a very good friend who helped me to study for many an exam. He was the least of my worries when it came to the risk of friendships. My other friends, including my fiancé, would be a different story. By becoming Christian, I would appear to be turning my back on them. Since my familial relationships were weak, what my friends thought was very important to me. I did not want to lose any of them. To be honest, even though my intellect had been influenced by my conversations with Therese, and by her example, I had not quite internalized what Christ was offering.

I was very much like the man who told Jesus, "I will follow you, Lord; but let me first say farewell to those at my home." Jesus answered, "No one who puts his hand to the plow and looks back is fit for the kingdom of God" (Lk 9:61-62). I had put my hands on the plow, but I kept looking back. Neither I nor the plow was going anywhere: I was weak and desperately needed grace.

13

Knocked Over by a Feather

Saint Augustine famously said that our hearts are restless until they rest in God. I discovered a related truth: The more I tried to push Christ back, the more restless my heart became.

The summer between my freshman and sophomore years started in the midst of all these conflicts in my mind and heart, but other pressing matters were vying for my attention. Since Alp was working at a university, he had more free time to spend in Ankara over the summer. During the previous months, he had also tutored an American. Raymond and his family had recently moved to Turkey from Texas. I had met them briefly before Alp and Raymond started to work together.

This kind man with salt-and-pepper hair had a wonderful impact on Alp. Both men were easygoing and intelligent with a similar sense of humor. I wish they had been able to spend more time together. Shortly after they started Turkish lessons, Alp moved to the Black Sea coast. Thankfully, he and Raymond stayed in touch for a while.

During that summer, Raymond and his wife, Agnes, invited us over for dinner. Agnes was as easygoing as her husband and very pleasant to be around. Alp and I enjoyed spending time at their place, where their four young children kept everyone down-to-earth. After more than fifteen years, I still remember the warmth their apartment offered to all who stepped inside. Many a night when I felt lonely or needed a Christian sanctuary, I found myself heading to their place. They graciously shared their precious American coffee and *Seinfeld* episodes. They often offered me their comfortable couch to sleep on. I am grateful for their hospitality and their humor.

The first visit in their home proved to be a perfect evening. Their kitchen window and balcony faced west, and a magnificent sunset provided the backdrop to our scrumptious dinner. Over freshly brewed coffee, the four of us talked about inconsequential things as the children wreaked harmless havoc around the house.

One of the remarkable things about that night, other than the company, was that Raymond mentioned that a family from Oklahoma had moved to Ankara recently and lived in a neighborhood not far from my campus. Jerome and Martha had two little boys, he said, and they were looking for someone to teach them Turkish. It would be different from tutoring an adult, because children learn through play and interaction. But since I was in a bit of a financial jam, this was a wonderful opportunity for me. I told Raymond that I had tutoring experience and was perfect for the job. Nothing like shameless self-promotion.

~

Soon afterward, Jerome and Martha were happy to give me a chance to see if I could get along with their children, Peter and Paul. The timing was so propitious that I was filled with gratitude, even though I did not know whom I should thank. I gently pushed away any thoughts of answered prayers or trusting someone bigger than myself. As far as I was concerned, it was just another job, and all the concerns about Christ and Christianity had left the country with Therese and Francis. I just wanted to finish college and to get on with my life.

I started seeing Peter and Paul twice a week beginning in September, and they provided a challenge for me. I had not spent much time with children, aside from some baby-sitting. But a babysitter needs only to make sure the children are alive when the parents get home. A good babysitter tries to connect with her charges and entertain them, but doing so is not required. Tutoring, on the other hand, demands productive and usually planned interaction. To do a good job with Peter and Paul was going to stretch me in new directions.

In fact, Peter and Paul opened a completely new door for me, a door no grown-up could have opened. Their general cuteness was, of course, overwhelming. Peter, the younger son, started to call me Tuna in a terribly charming manner, most likely because of my too Turkish name. In observing Therese's children, I had noticed the positive impact made by their Christian upbringing, but being a self-indulgent young adult, I did not make much of an effort to get to know them. Having matured a little more by the age of twenty-two and being compelled to form a relationship with Peter and Paul, I was even more struck by the difference that grace and for-giveness can make in a family. But my stubborn heart still had some distance to travel.

As my second year at the university started, things looked rather different from the previous year. I was now living in a dorm room with three other girls (coed dorms are not permitted in Turkey) instead of in my fiancé's apartment. I was teaching two little boys instead of an intellectual woman. More importantly, I was not as far away from God. The seeds of doubt sown by Therese and by Dostoyevsky's wonderful parable had brought me to a completely new spot in regard to religion. As Saint Thomas Aquinas declared in delight: "Grace is nothing else than a beginning of glory in us."[1]

In my blindness I did not see it at the time, but grace was already working within me. For a long time, it was bringing me closer to God. Even though I thought my world was falling apart around me, something new was being built out of the ruins. Everything I perceived as a disaster would turn out to be a blessing. My changing circumstances allowed me more freedom to follow where reason was leading me. I did not have the emotional and financial constraints of living with my fiancé. I was more independent. Additionally, over the years, grace and Therese's persistent appeals to reason and faith had transformed the hard soil of my soul into the good soil that allows the Word of God to take root and bear fruit (see Mt 13:8).

Therefore, when I began spending time with Peter and Paul in the fall of 2002, my heart and my mind were more receptive to the good news of salvation in Christ than they had ever been. Therese had made sure over the years that I knew the life of Christ as it was recorded in the New Testament. Jerome and Martha had a different mission, since they would be the ones to show what it means to live as a Christian.

Working with their children further exposed me to Christian family life. As with Therese's children, I could tell that

[1] Aquinas, *Summa Theologica*, II-II, 24, 3, trans. Fathers of the English Dominican Province, Christian Classics Ethereal Library, http://www.ccel.org/c cel/aquinas/summa.SS_Q24_A3.htm.

Peter and Paul felt secure in their identity and were free to explore the world in that security. They were two and five years old, and they naturally created plenty of mess and noise, despite Jerome's best efforts to keep the apartment immaculate. He and his best friend, "Val" the vacuum cleaner, worked overtime to keep up with the little ones. But in the midst of the hurly-burly of making sure that the children were fed and did not die in freak accidents, there was an abundance of joy and peace. I could not help but observe that the children did not fear their parents as I had feared mine. They did not lie or otherwise deceive in order to get out of trouble, as I had. In this special home, there was the healthy amount of fear that comes from respecting parents and dreading to disappoint them. Peter and Paul knew that their parents loved them and that they were fair and just when they disciplined them.

Jerome and Martha's marriage was another mystery to me. Until then, the only marriages I had witnessed were either broken or wounded by hurt and division. Even though I had come to know Therese and Francis well over the years, I had not observed their married life in its daily rhythm. Jerome and Martha, on the other hand, were like an open book to me as I spent time in their home with their sons. Jerome was unlike any husband I had ever seen. He was truly devoted to his wife and children.

Hierarchy is a crucial part of marriage and family life in Turkey. Many men see themselves as the absolute authority in their households. Even when men are not tyrannical, they do not share everything openly with their wives or treat them as their equals. There are always secrets, and there is always a game of power. Turkish sitcoms portray the father as a figure of authority who does not know what is happening in his household, while the mother is shown as the power behind the throne. In order to keep peace in the family and also to get what she wants, the wife and mother manipulates and lies. It is like the relationship between the sultan and his vizier. Obviously, real life is slightly different from sitcoms, but the underlying expectation in Turkish society is that husbands and wives do not work together to run their families.

Martha and Jerome's relationship, however, looked very different from the typical Turkish marriage. Jerome was neither the authoritarian but clueless man of Turkish sitcoms nor the weak, lazy slob of American TV. He was first and foremost a caring, respectful husband. He often praised Martha and tried to be as supportive as possible throughout the day. He helped around the house whenever he could. He did not act as though he expected Martha to serve him, as if her sole purpose in life was to please him. Instead, he anticipated every opportunity to serve her, the rest of his family, and others. Even though I had been blessed to have several wonderful Turkish men in my life and was never oppressed emotionally, neither Enver nor Alp had treated me in the strong, gentle, generous way in which Jerome treated Martha.

In the same manner, Martha showed love and respect for Jerome. She never used manipulation, the silent treatment, or emotional blackmailing. Instead, like her husband, she strove to serve others, especially her family. She never said a bad word about her husband; she made sure to praise him to his face and often when others were present. It was obvious that she trusted him completely. She was confident that Jerome would be there when she needed him. Martha reciprocated his reliability, by being a cheerful, joyful, caring wife and mother.

Here was a couple who understood and took to heart one of the most controversial verses in the New Testament:

Be subject to one another out of reverence for Christ.
Wives, be subject to your husbands, as to the Lord. For
the husband is the head of the wife as Christ is the head
of the Church, his body, and is himself its Savior. As the
Church is subject to Christ, so let wives also be subject in
everything to their husbands. Husbands, love your wives,
as Christ loved the Church and gave himself up for her, that
he might sanctify her, having cleansed her by the washing
of water with the word, that he might present the Church
to himself in splendor, without spot or wrinkle or any such
thing, that she might be holy and without blemish. Even so
husbands should love their wives as their own bodies. He
who loves his wife loves himself. (Eph 5:21–28)

I did not recognize it at the time, but what was clearly
missing in all my relationships was Christ. When a mere
human being is the most important person in one's life, all
involved suffer. It is too heavy a burden to expect someone
to fulfill all our needs. We are not created to be everything
for others. We are created to be partners, not owners. When
spouses operate selfishly and desire to have all their needs
met by another human being, they set themselves up for disappointment and resentment because no human being can
meet all one's needs. Jerome and Martha and Therese and
Francis let Christ love them first. Only then could they have
Christ-like love for their spouses and children. They were
sons and daughters of God first; then came all their other
roles. As they found fulfillment in their Lord, they found
satisfaction and joy in all the other parts of their lives. Their
world was ordered, and the source of that order was the
source of my confusion.

Little by little, seeing these flesh-and-blood examples of
Christian living, I found that grace became almost tangible.
The more time I spent in Martha and Jerome's home, the
more I wanted to go back. I accepted every invitation they

extended, and I worked with Peter and Paul as much as I could. I do not know if my company was as agreeable to them as theirs was to me, but they were gracious enough to share their family, their joy, and their love with me. In just a month, Jerome and Martha gave me a family. Their witness demonstrated to me what the grace of God was capable of, as the *Catechism of the Catholic Church* states:

> In order that the message of salvation can show the power of its truth and radiance before men, it must be authenticated by the witness of the life of Christians. "The witness of a Christian life and good works done in a supernatural spirit have great power to draw men to the faith and to God."[2]

To have a life like Jerome and Martha's, I needed only to reach up and grab the supernatural for myself. Ivan's parable had taught me that even though I was sinful, I had the free will to do something about it. As much as God wanted to save me, He would never force me to accept His hand. After all, it was a gift.

[2] CCC 2044, quoting Second Vatican Council, Decree on the Apostolate of the Laity *Apostolicam Actuositatem*, November 18, 1965, no. 6.

14

Holding On like a Bulldog

I was at a crossroads. For many days and nights, I thought about Christ and what it meant to be a Christian in Turkey. My pride, my selfishness, and my fears were so strong and confusing that I could not make a decision, even though I was all but convinced that Christ was the Son of God. Do I pick the road less traveled that leads to eternal life, or do I keep following the crowd? It did not help that the road to Christ was so little traveled in modern Turkey that I did not know any Turkish Christians. I was afraid of being alone in this journey. I was afraid of losing Alp. I was afraid of the reactions of my friends. I was afraid of not being able to get a respectable job. I was afraid of how unpredictable the future might become. I was very afraid.

There is a reason the phrase "Do not be afraid" is used rather frequently in the Scriptures: The Lord knows that we are afraid.

I was standing at this crossroads a little hazy because of restless nights and unfocused days. I could not move; my feet were heavier than ever. I needed yet another gentle nudge, and the Holy Spirit sighed and obliged.

I could walk from my dorm to my university department in about ten minutes through the beautiful campus, which looked even more appealing decorated with October foliage. On my way to an early-morning class, I slowly followed the familiar path without much thought. Few students were about at that hour. As I approached my destination, I suddenly saw a very brief scene in my mind's eye. I am not sure if it was a vision or a daydream, but it was as vivid as the concrete building towering in front of me.

My vision's setting was also outdoors, but it was somewhere else. There was a backdrop of snowy mountains and a cloudless blue sky. It seemed like a spring day; the atmosphere was fresher and more alive than the fall air I was breathing. The only person in the scene was a little girl sitting on the grass, seemingly preoccupied with the toys in front of her. She did not appear to be an important character, as she was tiny compared with the mountains and the meadow leading up to them. The girl had long dark hair like mine and was wearing a simple white dress. Suddenly, two giant hands came down from the heavens and offered the busy girl a present. The owner of the hands was so big that only His hands could be seen. The present He held out to the little girl was beautiful beyond description. It was wrapped exquisitely and had a glow so bright that it was almost too hard to look upon. In an instant I knew that this gift was something beyond any mortal's imagination and was much more valuable and important than anything man could possess. After a while, the little girl looked up and saw the dazzling gift that had come down from the skies. She thought for a moment and then said: "No, thank you, I have these toys to play with."

"Unbelievable!" I thought. "Silly little girl!" I wanted to say. "How could you possibly compare your petty little toys with that gift? How could you refuse such a splendid present? Do you not see that your life will be changed forever?" I felt like reaching into the vision and slapping some sense into this clueless child. But soon after these questions erupted in my mind, I realized that the little girl was none other than me. I was the one who was utterly preoccupied with life's little worries, missing the big picture and thinking that what I saw in front of me was all that there ever could be. I was the one who took forever to notice that somebody had been trying to get my attention for a very long time. I was the one who was afraid to lose her career and friends, which were pathetic in comparison with what God was offering me. I was the one who had refused the divine gift.

All of this took place in a span of a few seconds. The Holy Spirit had given me a little shove at the crossroads, making it clear which path to take. Choosing the same path as that little girl meant a life of earthly security and comfort, but what was that compared with eternal life? In that moment I decided to accept the magnificent gift and open it layer by layer for the rest of my life, trusting that one day I would see the owner of those hands face-to-face. This hope welled up so strongly in my soul that I did not care how narrow the gate was or how little traveled the road. Then and there I put my hand to the plow again and started pushing, and this time I was not looking back.

With this new resolution in my heart, it was a brand-new day for me, even as I went about doing what I ordinarily did. I experienced a lightness of being, and the things that would normally have caused me anxiety failed to pull me down. Classes were less stressful, friends less overwhelming, rain less annoying. The irksome things in daily life shrank as the truly wonderful things expanded. The world appeared more colorful, just as *Knight Rider* did the first time I watched it in color instead of in black and white. Everything around me seemed to have more depth, as if I were watching *Knight Rider* in 3-D. Behold, God was making everything new (see Rev 21:5)!

~

The following day, I went to work with Peter and Paul. After the lesson, as usual, Martha offered me coffee and whatever tasty goodies she had whipped up that day. As I sat at their kitchen table and watched her wash the dishes, I was at an unusual loss for words. I finally gave up trying to come up with the best way to explain my epiphany and said: "I think today is a wonderful day to become a Christian." It was October 2002, less than two months after I met Jerome, Martha, and their beautiful children, less than six months since they moved to Turkey. God works in mysterious ways.

Martha dropped the dish she was washing and turned around, not believing her ears. I definitely owed her an explanation. Soon after Jerome joined us in the kitchen, I told them in detail about Therese, Ivan, their witness to grace, and my daydream, or vision, of the little girl. They quietly listened as I narrated how agony and confusion had stalled me for a long time. Finally, when I finished my long-winded account, they offered to say "the prayer" with me. For Evangelical Protestants, saying this prayer is the means by which a person accepts Christ into his heart as his personal Lord and Savior. We prayed, we cried, and we had more coffee. It proved to be a long night of sharing and talking. I was a new creation, and I could not wait to learn all about my new life. When my journey began, I was a reluctant traveler like Bilbo Baggins, who was jostled and annoyed by uninvited guests in his house. That evening I made the same discovery eventually made by Bilbo—that I was being led on a thrilling, life-changing adventure.

After that day, I became the Sisyphus whose curse was lifted. No longer was I pushing a boulder up a hill, watching it fall back down and pointlessly repeating the process the next day. The restless, sleepless nights of indecisiveness were replaced with carefree dreams of a promising future. As the cliché aptly states, it was the beginning of the rest of my life. When I woke the day after having told Jerome and Martha, all I wanted to do was to learn more and more about this Christ who seemed to have changed my life forever. Thanks to Therese, I had already read quite a bit of the Bible, especially the Gospels, and I was familiar with Christian morality. So I began reading any Christian material, fiction or nonfiction I could get my hands on. The way of life that promoted selflessness and sacrifice was refreshing and exhilarating. It was like finding a cool oasis in the middle of a desert, and I could not drink enough.

~

As a neophyte Christian, I first wanted to explore Christianity from an insider's perspective. Soon after my conversion, Jerome started a Bible study with two other new believers. We met once a week at Jerome and Martha's home, and I became more and more familiar with Scripture. Other than preparing for the weekly Bible studies, I kept reading about Christian living. Thankfully, by then I knew enough believers to keep me supplied with books to read and movies to watch. It was as if I had a fire blazing in my mind, and I needed to keep it burning by constantly feeding it fuel.

I could not wait to express dying to myself and being born

anew in baptism. Although the concept of sacraments was foreign to me, and in a way I did not quite understand the meaning of baptism beyond its symbolism, it was clear that this would be a crucial step in my journey. That much was clear in the Bible. It would be a full-immersion baptism, as is practiced by most Evangelical Protestants. After the leaders of the Turkish congregation made sure that I was not a fake convert, a small group of friends and I gathered at the back of the church, where there was a tiny pool for baptisms.

It was May, so it was still a little cold, but no one cared. Jerome was to baptize me and bring me formally into God's family. In a plain dark T-shirt and shorts, I stepped into the little pool that came barely up to my waist. Following a few words about the importance of baptism and my journey, Jerome dunked me under the water three times in the name of the Father and of the Son and of the Holy Spirit. I slipped a little but thankfully did not color the baptismal water with my blood. I emerged, cleansed from my sins, and I felt happy and light. The congregants did not believe that my baptism washed my sins away. From their point of view, my sins had been removed when I confessed Jesus as Lord. The baptism was only the public witness to an event that had already occurred. No matter. A baptism is a baptism, and I was from that point forward a member of the Body of Christ. We had lunch in one of the two Chinese restaurants in Ankara. That night I went to bed with a renewed appreciation of how much God knew us, loved us, and took care of us.

~

A crucial need I had at the time was to meet other Turkish Christians. Since I was still a hopeless geek, meeting new people did not come easily to me, especially so soon after my life-changing decision. Jerome and Martha put me in touch with some members of the largest Turkish Protestant church in the city, who also held weekly meetings for young Turkish believers. I had never been to a Turkish church. Many times I attended services at the International Church, on Sundays and on Christmas and Easter. I had thought my experience of conversion was so rare that I would forever remain an oddity in my own country. Thankfully, this would not be the case.

The Turkish couple who ran the weekly meetings also worked for an organization that focused on evangelizing college students. They were not only young and approachable but also accustomed to being among the few Christians on a university campus. I shall call them Bora and Ada. When I showed up in their apartment for the first time during a cold central-Anatolia winter, I was not aware that their home and friendship would be a refuge for many years to come. Becoming part of the group that met weekly was not as hard as I had predicted. Bora and Ada welcomed Jerome, Martha, and me to their cozy and tastefully decorated apartment with delicious homemade goodies. It was what every college student craved. We shared the happenings of our lives over endless cups of tea and cookies and talked about God and where we were in our journeys into His kingdom. Of course, we prayed for each other, for we needed prayer most of all. After each meeting, I couldn't wait for the next one. It was a fellowship unlike any I had experienced.

Ada and I slowly became good friends as we spent more and more time together. She was raised a Christian as her father was a convert. She grew up going to church every

Sunday and attending the only Turkish Christian camp for children every year. She was much more settled in her faith than I was. She was nurturing, intuitive, and a wonderful cook. What more did I want? I just loved sipping the English tea she brewed and nibbling her baked wonders as I vented about the people and incidents in my life. She was a good listener, and she always had some wisdom to offer. She became like a sister to me.

Bora, on the other hand, became the older brother I never had. We quibbled frequently. We constantly tried to outdo each other in sarcasm. Bora loved reading and challenging himself. The three of us would spend many hours talking about movies, theology, and other topics of common interest. After Jerome and Martha's, their home became yet another familiar destination. My family was getting bigger and bigger as I learned about Christ. Little by little, my anxieties and fears were being replaced by the confidence and the hopefulness that come with being part of a community.

As I learned more about Christianity and the Bible, some nagging questions started to bug me. Two beliefs that bothered me were creationism and *sola scriptura*, which is the Protestant doctrine that the Bible is the supreme and only authority in matters of faith and practice. Neither belief made sense to me, but instead of trying to reconcile the conflicting thoughts in my head, I told them to shut up. It worked. Once in a while these annoying contradictions would reemerge and have the effect of a pebble in my shoe, but I would sing louder and plug my ears. I kept reassuring myself that clearly I had a long way to go before I could truly comprehend these sensitive and seemingly problematic issues. Until such a time that I could fully understand and accept these teachings, I thought, all I needed to do was to sweep my doubts under the carpet and stomp on them until the bump was flat.

My personal life was changing, too. Alp would still come to Ankara to see me every other weekend. Before my conversion he was aware that something was bothering me deeply. Even though we did not see each other daily, we made sure to talk several times a day. During his first visit after my conversion, I told him that I had become a Christian. I was very afraid of his reaction, because he was still very precious to me. After agonizing for days about how best to break the news to him, I was utterly underwhelmed by his reaction, in a good way. He was neither mad nor happy. He simply said that he would love me no matter what and that my faith was of no consequence. I was very relieved to hear those words, as I was sure that it would be he who would have trouble with my faith, not I who would be troubled by his lack of faith. It would be a while before I realized that we were not right for each other.

As my circle of Christian friends grew, I had less desire to spend time with my atheist friends. Not that I did not like them anymore, but with every passing day I had less in common with them. I did not want to sit around making fun of God. Getting drunk and partying no longer appealed to me. Many evenings, I cut short my time with friends at a bar or a nightclub so that I could go to a Bible study. At times, I felt I was being pulled in opposite directions, but not with equal force. Gradually I drifted away from my former friends and Alp, without even realizing it.

Either Alp noticed that I was not the same girl anymore, or he was not as comfortable with my becoming a Christian as he said he was. Maybe it was a combination of the two. Regardless, he started to act very differently from the man

I had known before. Undoubtedly, the biggest change was my decision to stop having sexual relations until we were married. Even though, after the abortion, I subconsciously tried to stay away from the act that led to pregnancy, unsurprisingly my declaration to live according to Christian sexual morality upset Alp.

We were drifting apart. Even the books I read and the music I listened to widened the separation between us. On the weekends when he came to Ankara, Alp noticed that I was talking more and more about people he didn't know. Having been together for a long time, we knew each other's friends. Or rather, we used to. I invited Alp to a few Christian gatherings while he was in town, but he vehemently refused to be a part of my "cult" even when it meant free food. Watching me slip away from him and feeling powerless to do anything to stop it, Alp became first defensive and then hostile. He even distanced himself from his Christian friend Raymond.

Months passed as we tried to find common ground and to make our relationship work. In hindsight, however, I am not sure I wholeheartedly wanted to continue the engagement. On my part, the abortion had already severed some of the connection between us. A little tear had been made in the fabric of our love, and it would eventually spoil the whole piece of cloth. Also, I wanted to be with someone who shared my beliefs, especially now that my faith in Christ had become the most important thing in my life. I had the same perspective when I was an atheist. Dating a Muslim or a Christian then would have been inconceivable. It was extremely difficult for me not to be able to talk about the new things I was learning or to discuss an obscure theological point with the man I was planning to spend the rest of my life with. I wanted someone to share my doubts as well as my joys; someone who would lift me up when I fell. I did not want to mean everything to him. I wanted for us to walk toward God together, instead of becoming each other's god.

The friction between Alp and me became unbearable and irreversible, and a mere six months from the day I expressed to Martha my desire to become a Christian, we broke up. I was both sad and relieved. I grieved that a man with whom I spent so much of my life would be gone. Worse yet, he might be lost to Christ for good. All I could do was hope that Raymond's time with Alp would eventually bear some fruit, and that grace would eventually overwhelm him. At the same time, I was relieved because the days of constantly defending my decision or completely ignoring the topic were over. I did not have to dread the phone calls or the fortnightly visits. I could take a deep breath and keep exploring the ocean I had discovered.

Thereafter, my identity became more tied to Christ than anyone else. I became more involved in different ministries and felt more a part of the Christian community than before. I owe much to Ada and Bora for this. They always made sure that I was invited and felt welcomed, and they introduced me to lots of other Christians. They led me to what would become the most important ministry in my life, which would eventually lead me home to the Roman Catholic Church.

15

Rebuilding Burned Bridges

My relationship with Alp was not the only one that was affected by my conversion. The broken bond between my parents and me troubled me more and more. Honoring my father and mother was one of the last things I wanted to do. Every time I thought about either of them, I kept recalling all the wrongs they had done to me and my brother. My record keeping was impeccable. As much as I wanted to avoid the subject entirely, the Holy Spirit whispered louder and louder until the stubbornness in me started to yield. But I did not know how to begin to mend these relationships, especially with my father, from whom I had not heard for years.

Unable to silence the nagging of the Holy Spirit, I finally sought advice from someone much wiser than I—Jerome. When I told him of my desire to mend fences with my father, Jerome asked, "Have you tried praying for him?"

Um, no, I have not.

"It's the way to forgiveness," he said. I was really suspicious about the effectiveness of prayer because it was hard for me to erase the traces of atheistic skepticism. In this case, I had no idea how praying would help me to forgive my father.

By this time, I had been a Christian for more than a year, yet prayer did not come to me easily. It still doesn't. I set an alarm to remind myself to pray or go to bed late to finish the half-said Rosary, while trying not to fall asleep. The first time I went to a meeting with Turkish Christians, they all bowed their heads to pray as I sat straight in my seat. At first, I refused to bow my head or show any other sign of humility. Slowly and patiently the Lord worked on my pride until I was able to bow my head when we prayed. But the idea that praying for my father would help me to forgive him did not make sense. After all, what had he done to deserve my prayers?

Regardless of my skepticism, I decided to give Jerome's idea a try. The first night, in my dorm room, I put away my Bible, folded my hands, and tried to pray for my father, who I felt had never been a father to me.

Not a word came from my lips. I could not utter one word on his behalf. So hardened was my heart toward him that I could not even say something along the lines of, "Lord, let him have a peaceful night's sleep." Nope, he did not deserve peaceful sleep tonight or ever.

I tried again the following night, and still not a word. Not the night after that, nor the night after that could I pray for him. The more I wanted to pray for my father and could not, the more I realized how much my hatred of him had harmed me instead of harming him. I can't remember where I heard this saying, but it came back to me then: Refusing to forgive is like drinking poison and hoping that the other person will die. My inability to pray for my father showed me how unforgiveness had poisoned my heart.

It took more than a week, but I finally asked the Lord to give my father a good night's sleep. After that night, praying for him got a bit easier. I prayed a little more for him every night, until I could finally pray for his current marriage. The more the words of prayer poured out of my mouth, the more the poison inside me was withdrawn. It was a slow process, but the more I saw how broken my father was, how he was yet another sinner in dire need of Christ's forgiveness, the more the darkness in my heart was overcome. At last I could believe that if God could forgive him, so could I.

Months passed as I prayed for my father and my mother, so that there could be some kind of reconciliation. As the end of my senior year was approaching, the graduation ceremony seemed to be a good occasion for both of them to come and see me. I tracked down my father's number and asked him if he would be willing to celebrate that happy day with me. The phone conversation was as awkward as expected, because we hadn't talked for years. I tried very hard not to say the things that had come to mind numerous times, such as "I did it all without you" or "You don't actually deserve to be part of my life." By the grace of God, my tongue did not betray me and my pride did not get the best of me.

In return, there was a humility in my father's voice that I had never heard before. The man who had always blamed others for the things that went wrong in his life and who hoped his young children would carry the burden of the relationship was gone. He said he would be honored to witness this accomplishment. It was a short, emotional conversation, but it lifted a weight off my heart.

∽

On the day of the graduation ceremony, I picked up my parents and my brother from the intercity bus terminal and took them to the apartment where I was house-sitting for the summer. Did I mention that the phone conversation with my father was awkward? It was nothing compared with the morning we gathered as a family for the first time since my father left more than twelve years ago. I cooked them breakfast, and we all enjoyed a peaceful meal on the balcony that overlooked the city. Neither of my parents knew why, after all these years, I had decided to reach out to them. I knew, however, that it was time for me to give credit where credit was due. My parents had given me my life.

After breakfast, I told my parents that I needed to talk to them. In Turkish culture, people try to avoid conflict until everyone involved explodes. Honest, heart-to-heart talks are very rare, and they are even rarer when the one who is giving the talk is younger than the ones who are receiving it. My father sat on a chair farthest from where I was standing, and my mother leaned against the countertop. My brother was taking a nap. Against all our cultural taboos, my opening line was far from being sugarcoated: "If it weren't for Christ, I would not want anything to do with you." My mother came to stand next to me to indicate that the only guilty one in the room was my father. "You, too," I told her, putting a little distance between us to show that they were in the same boat as far as I was concerned.

For the next fifteen minutes, I told them how much they had hurt and scarred me by leaving, not caring, and physically and emotionally abusing me. If my life hadn't changed drastically two years before, my only desire would have been to cut off ties with both of them. My mother seemed shocked, since in her delusion she kept telling herself that she was the perfect parent because she hadn't left us. As long as she stayed with us, she thought, it didn't matter how we were raised. My father, on the other hand, started to cry a few minutes after the beginning of my talk. I had known that he had changed through the years, because he had been nothing but humbled since my first phone call, but I did not expect tears. Finally, I explained that I had become a Christian and that Christ was asking me to forgive them just as He had forgiven me.

I could tell that they weren't happy that I had left the Muslim faith they had tried to instill in me. But at the same time, they knew that their only daughter would be lost to them without Christ. Not being able to keep his composure, my father went out to the balcony and cried for hours until we were ready for the ceremony. He was nothing like the man I remembered. The Holy Spirit had given me a new perspective, and from this point of view, I saw a man who was crumbling under the weight of his own decisions and sins. As I watched him cry, trying to hide his tears from all of us, the last drops of poison left my soul, and finally I forgave my father. After that day, my relationship with him improved. The lost years would not be restored, but at least we could begin again.

My mother never afterward mentioned that day or the talk we had, or showed any sign of remorse. It didn't matter. If there was anything I had learned during those nights when I could not pray, it was that forgiveness did not depend on the apology or the remorse of the other person. It was about sharing an infinitesimal fraction of the love that Christ has shown me. Mending the relationship was hard without my mother's cooperation, and we stayed at a level that was suggestive of duty rather than unconditional love, but at least the Lord had given me the grace to move beyond past resentments.

Not once was my Christianity mentioned after that day. It was the proverbial elephant in the room. My mother and my brother attended the nuptial Mass that united me and my husband, but my father excused himself by saying that his bus would arrive too late. That was all right with me. I continue to hope and to pray that my life will witness Christ to them even if we never talk about Him.

~

A few months after receiving my bachelor's degree, I started to work toward a master's in history. Bilkent University would be my new home, and I would need to make new friends, Christian or otherwise. I wanted to live and to study on campus, which meant that I had less and less contact with Therese, Martha, Ada, and their families. I was a little scared to be far from all the good influences in my life. I feared that it would be all too easy for me to lose my way without other Christians to encourage me along the right path. I had heard that many Turkish converts drift away from Christianity after being baptized. In fact, in Turkey three out of four newly baptized Christians do not continue to live Christian lives. I wanted to be part of the 25 percent who keep the faith. And so it would come to pass.

During my first year at Bilkent, God provided me with supportive Christian friends. When I met Irene and John, they were living on campus because John taught advanced English. I began meeting weekly with Irene and learned to trust her wisdom and to appreciate her gentle nature. Soon we were spending evenings watching *The Simpsons* and *The Lord of the Rings* while enjoying chocolate and coffee. I felt very at home around Irene and John, and I spent so many nights on their couch that I started to call it my husband.

During my second year, I met Clare, who had recently

moved to Turkey to earn her master's in international relations at Bilkent. Between Irene and Clare, I had a wonderful support network and a weekly Bible study. As I moved from one adventure to another and continued my wanderings, the Lord never neglected to put godly women in my path.

It was also during this time that my journey toward the Catholic Church began.

16

Reading Cardinal Ratzinger

During the first summer after I became a believer, I started volunteering as a counselor in Christian summer camps. I worked at a camp for Third Culture Kids, which is a term used to refer to children who were raised in a culture different from that of their parents for a significant part of their formative years. Following that two-week camp at the base of Mount Olympus, I took a bus to a summer camp for Turkish Christian teenagers. The arduous overnight trip from the Mediterranean coast to the Aegean coast followed the path of one of Saint Paul's missionary journeys.

The teen site was built and owned by Koreans, who would let the place out for various Christian events, such as conferences, retreats, and camps. It was a blessing to have a facility all to ourselves. It was even more of a blessing to be settled along the walls of the ancient city of Ephesus. The campers were exposed to its beauty in addition to its historical and religious significance.

Even though I was exhausted from the bus ride and the previous weeks of keeping up with teenagers, I was very happy to be part of this ministry. It allowed high school students to fellowship with people who shared their beliefs. With so few Turks identifying as Christian, peers and role models are very precious and rare. This camp was the only nationwide one for high school students. For many it was the only opportunity to meet with Christian friends throughout the year.

Being in high school is hard enough; being a follower of Christ in high school does not exactly put you on the popular list. The camp helped high school students to understand why they should be willing to suffer for Christ—not because their parents did, but because they themselves chose to follow Christ. Given the raging hormones in any normal adolescent, many might argue that it was not a very good idea to put a hundred high schoolers together for a week and see what happens. But for those of us who worked there, the risks were worth the rewards. We felt privileged to offer our labor of love for their chance to grow in their faith.

Bora, Ada, and a few others from Ankara were the ones who put this event together. After surviving the week-long insanity without any permanent damage, I was asked if I would be willing to help with the almost year-long preparations for the next round. After two seconds of consideration, I accepted. It felt wonderful to be part of something much bigger than myself. The teen camp became the source of many friendships and joyful days, and it eventually led me to the man who helped me across the Tiber.

I met Anthony at the second teen camp I attended. He had been raised in Istanbul by "worker" parents who had been living in Turkey for decades. He was studying international relations at the University of Notre Dame, and he was as laid-back as they come. He was a natural with the teenagers, possibly because he had never outgrown his own teenager spirit. As we worked together through the challenges of adolescent hormones mixed with existential crises, we became very good friends. Even though he was two years younger than I, we finished our bachelor's degrees around the same time because of my lost college years in Istanbul. As I began my master's degree, Anthony was pursuing a job in Istanbul as a journalist.

As already mentioned, I began my graduate studies at Bilkent University in Ankara, a few miles up the road from my previous school. Even though the campuses were almost adjacent to each other, the universities were markedly different. Bilkent is among the best private universities in Turkey. Unlike at Middle East Tech, the campus environment sported expensive cars and brand-name purses. Because of the wealth of its paying undergraduate students, the graduate school generously pays the tuition of its graduate students and offers them free dorm rooms and a monthly stipend. A master of arts degree in history takes three years to acquire at Bilkent. During my second year in the program, I met with Anthony for lunch on a warm autumn day in Istanbul. My agnostic roommate from Bilkent joined us.

By this time, Anthony and I had known each other for about four years. We stayed in regular communication because we had shared responsibilities for the teen camps. As we talked about skits, improv sessions, and other activities, we became kindred spirits. This friendship was probably why he was a little hesitant about sharing his life-changing news at the little family restaurant where we had lunch. After the small talk, Anthony said, "I have something to tell you, but don't be upset."

I graciously replied, "As long as you are not pregnant, I'll be all right."

Thankfully he was not pregnant. He smiled and continued with a mixture of reluctance and hesitation.

"I became a Catholic," he said.

I wished he were pregnant.

I could not believe my ears. How could he do this? How dare he side with those who believed in such weird and corrupted things as saints and purgatory? How could he accept the infallibility of the pope, a mere man? Also, what about all that idolatrous stuff about Mary? How could I forget all the awful things the Catholic Church did, such as the Crusades and the Inquisition? What was happening?

Needless to say, I was hysterical.

My agnostic roommate was surely amused when she saw me become slightly unraveled at Anthony's news. Poor Anthony should have thought to wear chainmail and armor and to bring his shield for deflecting my reaction. Lacking such protection, he tried to answer a few of my questions while ducking under the table. I was sad, frustrated, and concerned for my friend. As we concluded our lunch, all I wanted to do was to help him. But clearly, holding him by the shoulders and shaking very hard was not going to work. I would have to come up with a more cunning plan.

I was in Istanbul for a conference with my history department and returned to Ankara shortly after this exchange with Anthony. Before I devised a plan to save my friend from the fiery clutches of the papists, I received a package in the mail. Having anticipated my reaction to his conversion, Anthony had sent me a book with a note: "So that you know I haven't completely lost my mind." *We shall see, my good man. We shall see.*

At first glance, it was an ugly little book written by a man I had never heard of: Mark Shea. The cover was brown with a navy blue title: *By What Authority? An Evangelical Discovers Catholic Tradition.* The book felt light in my hands, and I could not imagine how it could have changed Anthony so much. I resented the betrayal of the man who wrote it.

Really, Mr. Shea? You, too? I felt absolutely sure that I was correct about Catholicism and that my friend and Mr. Shea were wrong.

Thus, I set out to prove that Mr. Shea had misled Anthony. I was too proud to realize that my quest was absurd, given that I knew so little about the Scriptures, never mind the theology and the history of the Catholic Church. But my pride is a monster and not easily tamed or persuaded. I headed to our trusty library, which unsurprisingly had few books on Catholic or Protestant theology. The only relevant book I could find was Cardinal Joseph Ratzinger's *Principles of Catholic Theology*, the English version of his German book *Theologische Prinzipienlehre*. I carried the slightly intimidating volume to one of the library's wooden desks and eagerly opened it. I started to read what this Ratzinger person had to say and was struck right away by the fact that his writing is not for the faint of heart. It definitely was over the head of a novice Protestant whose native tongue is not English. It was painful. In spite of the completely strange terminology, it was clear to me that the book was written by a very intelligent man whose prose was beyond my comprehension. I respectfully returned the book to its place and decided not to mess with Cardinal Ratzinger's written word until I knew a little more.

I wish someone had told me he was the pope.

Concluding that Mr. Shea would be a less formidable opponent than the German scholar, I decided to read the book Anthony sent me. Its little more than two hundred pages mostly deal with Sacred Tradition and where the Catholic Church claims to have gotten her authority.

In his book Shea points out the flaws in the Protestant idea of *sola scriptura*, that is, that the Bible is the sole authority for the Christian faith. He demonstrates that many cherished beliefs of Evangelicals and Catholics alike cannot be established by relying only on the Bible. The three major examples he gives are the sanctity of life as opposed to abortion, the exclusivity of marriage as opposed to polygamy, and the Trinitarian God as opposed to Arianism (an early heresy). He argues that without Scripture and Tradition, that is, the teachings Jesus gave His apostles, Christians would have insufficient grounds for adopting these doctrines. Shea explains that Christ Himself established the authority of His apostles over His Church, which He promised to protect until the end of time.

I learned from Shea that the Catholic Church's teachings on faith and morals have been passed down to us through apostolic succession; that is, the first apostles chose and taught their successors, who chose and taught their successors, and so on. The pope, who is the bishop of Rome, is the successor of Saint Peter. The other bishops are the successors of the other apostles. Together they have protected throughout the ages the deposit of faith entrusted to them by Christ. In fact, it was bishops who put the Bible together. They selected the writings that form the canon of Scripture, that is, the list of books included in the Bible.

To be honest, after reading Shea's book, I was not suddenly convinced of the Catholic Church's authority over all Christians, but I found a giant hole in my arguments against all things Catholic. Shea's book also made me realize how little I knew about Catholic history and theology. The history part was lopsided because I has grown up in a Muslim country. The theology part was lopsided because I was surrounded by Protestants who knew no more than I did. I had never met a devout Catholic, and many of the committed Christians around me were fiercely anti-Catholic. For instance, a Christian leader scolded me publicly for reading a book printed by a Catholic publisher. I had the book with me when I was working as an interpreter at a Christian conference. Printed on the spine of the book was a Chi-Rho, an early Christian symbol using the first two letters of the Greek word for Christ. The monogram caught the attention of one of the speakers, who pointed at me across a few tables and upbraided me for my choice of books: "Do you know what you're reading? Only Catholics use that symbol!" He made it sound as if I were reading something written by the Father of Lies himself.

For a long while after that encounter, I did not want to share my second thoughts about Protestant theology with anybody. Before muddying the waters with my mentors and friends, I wanted to make sure that the Catholic Church offered answers for the questions that had been nagging me since I had become a Christian.

For a time, the rug I had swept my questions under was heavy enough to hold them down. But as my faith matured and as more books on theology were added to my library, it became clear that Protestant teaching was not consistent on practical matters such as divorce and abortion or even on doctrinal matters such as the Trinity. Also, I had been unable to find a satisfactory and convincing argument in favor of *sola scriptura* or against the Church's Magisterium, the teaching authority composed of the pope and the other bishops. It was clear that the answers to my questions were to be found somewhere other than in the Protestant churches, if they could be found at all. I realized that three of the four matters that troubled me most were founding pillars of the Protestant movement; and I feared that if one crumbled, the whole thing would come tumbling down, and there would be nowhere else to go.

The mere fact that reading theology had become a major

interest of mine did not mean that understanding and en-
lightenment came easily. On the contrary, some points of
doctrine became more complex even as they became a little
clearer. My most troublesome Protestant notions, such as
sola fide (the belief that one is saved by faith alone), required
page after page of explanation to corroborate with the Bible.
It did not make sense to me that such an important aspect
of the faith would be this complicated. I lived for the sim-
pler things. Therefore, in the course of the few years that I
was a Protestant, I became convinced that many things were
amiss. Even though I was bothered by many inconsistencies
among Protestants, I was able to narrow my main objections
to four: *sola scriptura*, *sola fide*, the lack of a Magisterium, and
creationism.

From the beginning of my spiritual pilgrimage, I was quite
puzzled about the idea of relying on the Bible alone. It didn't
make sense, because the Bible as we know it was not com-
piled until centuries after Christ's Ascension. Did the early
Christians wander around aimlessly, hoping that one day
there would be a book that would guide them in their journey? How was it that Christ, who had given up His life to
save us from slavery to sin, would just leave without making
sure that there was a way for us to stay on the narrow path?
It made sense to me that He established an authority to lead
His flock. After all, Ivan Karamazov had taught me that human nature was not to be trusted and desperately needed
divine guidance.

Reading the Bible and relying on my own interpretation
as the Holy Spirit led me did not inspire confidence. Even
though I believed I was saved, it was pretty obvious that I
was still a sinner. Especially in important matters of faith,
how was it possible that every Christian could make up
his own mind, when his own intellect was not reliable? In

fact, the various Protestant churches were divided on these matters. If the indwelling of the Holy Spirit were enough to guide every believer to the truth about Christ, wouldn't every believer come to the same conclusions about Him? Either there was something deficient in the Holy Spirit, or there was something deficient in our human nature, and it seemed more likely that the fault was ours and not God's. If so, that conclusion necessarily raises a question: If human nature tends to get in the way of the truth, wouldn't Christ have known that and provided His Church with something to counteract that tendency?

The things that bothered me because a coherent body of Protestant teaching was lacking were not inconsequential aspects of Christian living, but matters that touch upon the very principles that ought to guide our actions. In one of the Bible studies I attended, the doctrine of the Trinity was questioned because the word "Trinity" itself is not in the Bible. I remember being particularly confused, because the Trinity is such a central piece of the Christian belief system, or so I thought. I met Christians who believed that abortion is acceptable because it is not explicitly banned by Christ. Yet abortion is a matter of life and death. Even if Christ never mentioned abortion, I could not believe that He would approve the killing of innocent unborn children. If the principles we need in order to see the evil of abortion are not spelled out in the Bible, how could the Bible alone be enough? I wondered.

Even *sola scriptura* is not in the Bible. The go-to verse for Protestants when this fact is pointed out is from the Second Letter of Paul to Timothy: "All Scripture is inspired by God and profitable for teaching, for reproof, for correction, and for training in righteousness, that the man of God may be complete, equipped for every good work" (3:16–17). But to me, these verses hinted that Scripture was a useful tool, rather than the sole source in matters of faith.

Furthermore, Saint Paul's discussion of Tradition was a little outside the box of *sola scriptura*. Whereas he could have said to follow the words of his letters, he urged the faithful to stay in line with the traditions they had been taught.[1] Either Paul was not aware that the traditions he kept talking about were not mentioned in the Bible, or there was a problem with the notion of Bible alone.

One last reason I was uneasy with *sola scriptura* was that I did not trust myself. How could I be sure that, try as I might, I would be able to interpret correctly what the Holy Spirit was trying to teach me? For that matter, without a divine guarantee, how could I trust anyone? I respected Jerome above anyone else in these matters, but how could I trust even his interpretation? After all, we still have to operate on this side of death. That means that we still sin.

Like *sola scriptura*, *sola fide* has no basis in the Bible or in common sense. Protestants and Catholics agree that we were all sinners and that sin created a chasm between God and us. As sinners, we had no means to cross or to fill up this chasm. It was Christ's sacrifice that bridged this gap. Grace alone, given by Christ, not our works, would save us. So far, so good: Protestants and Catholics are arm in arm about *sola gratia*. After that, however, things get a little compli-

---

[1] Here are some examples of his exhortations: "I commend you because you remember me in everything and maintain the traditions even as I have delivered them to you" (1 Cor 11:2). "Now we command you, brethren, in the name of our Lord Jesus Christ, that you keep away from any brother who is living in idleness and not in accord with the tradition that you received from us" (2 Thess 3:6). "So then, brethren, stand firm and hold to the traditions which you were taught by us, either by word of mouth or by letter" (2 Thess 2:15). "What you have heard from me before many witnesses entrust to faithful men who will be able to teach others also" (2 Tim 2:2).

cated. I was taught by the Protestants who led me to the doorstep of faith that once I was "saved", there was nothing I could do that would make myself "unsaved". There are many nuances among Protestants concerning salvation, but "faith alone" is as important as the "Bible alone".

But what would happen, I wondered, if I were to return to my utterly sinful life after having lived as a faithful Christian for years? Would I be on the road to hell, or since I was already saved, would I not have to worry about such a possibility? Some Christians told me that if I were genuinely saved, I would not go back to my sinful life. But who knows if his own conversion was genuine? And if my conversion was genuine, would it be impossible for me to sin? Did God take away my free will or my weak nature as soon as I said "the prayer"? Put another way, the answer intended to reassure me was that I would not desire to sin and to displease the Heavenly Father after having received the wonderful gift of salvation. Still, I was unconvinced. What if, in a moment of weakness, a genuine Christian committed adultery? Such a scenario did not seem far-fetched to me. Would that act not be a sin because it was committed by someone who had genuinely been saved?

Another consideration in the discussion about works is that many Scripture passages encourage Christ's followers to do good deeds, to be perfect and fruitful. If works were irrelevant for salvation, why would Christ and His apostles urge us to live holy lives? Christ said that barren branches would be cut off and thrown into fire. He did not say that these branches were not part of the tree from the beginning; He said that they failed to produce fruit (see Mt 3:10; 7:19). We become part of the Lord's Body and receive His grace in order to do the works He asks of us. They are His works, but He chooses to do them through us.

Another relevant verse is from the Letter of James, a New Testament epistle that Martin Luther wanted to delete from the Bible:

> You see that a man is justified by works and not by faith alone. And in the same way was not also Rahab the harlot justified by works when she received the messengers and sent them out another way? For as the body apart from the spirit is dead, so faith apart from works is dead. (2:24-26)

My third problem with Protestant theology was the lack of a Magisterium, or an authority under which all the faithful could be gathered. As I read the Bible, even to my untrained ears, it was clear that Christ could not have desired division among His followers. There are thousands of Protestant denominations, each one claiming to have the right doctrine. Surely, this chaos was not intended by the Person who created us and knows our rebellious nature better than we know ourselves. If God could become man and rise from the dead, why couldn't He give us an authority that He would protect from error? If Christ were not able to establish a Church that was invincible, then after all, maybe the Muslim claim that the faith had been corrupted is true.

Answering these questions, as if in anticipation of them, are the words of Jesus to Peter: "On this rock I will build my Church, and the gates of Hades shall not prevail against it" (Mt 16:18). That was a divine promise, and I was quite sure that we could count on God to keep His promises. By establishing a Church that was guided by the Holy Spirit, the Lord would solve the problems of disunity and heresy. Faith and morals would be protected under the divine seal. Really, how hard was it for the Creator of the universe to ensure that the Church He died for would stand until He returned?

Lastly, the creationist explanation of the origin of life

bothered me. I was willing to accept that the heavens and the earth might have been formed by God in a matter of days or that the earth is not as old as scientists say. But the desire to twist or to reject science so that it would correspond with a literal interpretation of the book of Genesis was problematic for me. Again, without a Magisterium, how did we even know which parts of the Bible to take literally and which parts figuratively? Surely, if there was an omniscient and omnipotent Being, He would be able to use any means to create life. Why couldn't He use a process of evolution? Evolution and God are not mutually exclusive.

Science and religion, though complementary, explore different spheres: Science can observe and measure only physical causes; religion concerns itself with the spiritual realm. Science can tell us what things are made of and how things work, but not the why. It can tell us that man is made of this and that, and that muscles work this way and not that way, but it cannot tell us why we exist in the first place, what our lives are for. Therefore, science cannot give us the principles we need to guide our actions. We must look elsewhere for those. By the same token, religion cannot tell us the size and the composition of a chicken egg or the speed of light. I respected what science had to offer and what its limits were. And I was relieved to discover that the Catholic Church does too. The Church does not read the book of Genesis as if it were a scientific text. She invites me to believe that God created everything and gave everything its design and purpose. She leaves me free to accept the theory of evolution. As Saint Thomas Aquinas said, one should not try to defend the Christian faith with arguments that are so patently opposed to reason that the faith is made to look ridiculous and deserving of scorn.

In the Catholic Church, I found room for a mutually

beneficial relationship with science. Pope John Paul II explained this relationship: "Science can purify religion from
error and superstition. Religion can purify science from idol-
atry and false absolutes. Each can draw the other into a wider
world. A world in which both can flourish."[2] This understanding of different realms was the answer to my discom-
fort with creationism. Because of my curiosity, my desire
for truth guided by grace, I had found Christ. Yet I did not
want to leave my intellect at the door of my faith and become the scorn of unbelievers. The Catholic Church in her
wisdom gave me a way to enter through the door with my
intellect intact.

To be honest, the theological arguments for Catholicism
were so strong that it did not take very long for me to become convinced that my path was gently but surely leading
to Rome. Once again, however, it was not my head holding
me back, but my heart: I did not want to create any problems with my newfound Christian family.

The last straw for me was reading about Martin Luther.
Just as Islam started to lose its appeal as I read the biography of Muhammad with an open mind, the warm glow of
Protestantism began to grow dim as I read a biography of
Martin Luther published by Penguin Press. Being afraid of
Catholic bias, I chose a title from a secular publisher that
was not affiliated with any particular church. The biography did not chronicle the life of a man who heroically stood
up against the establishment but the life of a man who was
used by those with political aspirations. Luther had problems
with some of the clergy and their practices that abused the

[2] John Paul II, Letter of His Holiness John Paul II to Reverend George V.
Coyne, S.J., Director of the Vatican Observatory (June 1, 1988), w2.vatican
.va/content/john-paul-ii/en/letters/1988/documents/hf_jp-ii_let_19880601_p
adre-coyne.html.

faithful, but he had an unstable mind and chose the wrong way to deal with his grievances and problems. Just like Muhammad, he was not a man I wanted to follow. I was disappointed beyond measure with his life, and I was upset that no Christian had encouraged me to investigate this hero of Protestantism and the champion of *sola scriptura*.

As I read about Luther's deranged views about Christ, demons, reason, sin, and faith, I could not believe that this man and I shared the same religion. Many Protestants argued in online forums that they were not Lutherans, so what he said was not binding for them. But at the same time, nobody could deny that the principles and the doctrines of Protestantism such as *sola scriptura* and *sola fide* were conjured up by this man. How could I trust the reasoning of a man who was willing to throw out the Letter of James because it did not fit into what he was preaching? I saw that if Christians accept Luther's views and move away from Rome on account of them, then they accept the idea that they are free to divide among themselves continually. What about Christ's prayer that His Church be one? "I in them and you in me, that they may become perfectly one, so that the world may know that you have sent me and have loved them even as you have loved me" (Jn 17:23). Even if there were abuses and wrongdoings by members of the Catholic Church, who would benefit from the division, suffering, and bloodshed caused by following in the footsteps of Martin Luther and others like him?

17

Jesuits in a Muslim Country

I was happy with my life in Protestant circles. I was part of
a good ministry serving high schoolers. I had a wonderful
Bible study group. Over the previous five years, between
2002 and 2007, I had made very good friends. But the more
I read about Catholicism, the more I realized that the answers to my questions were found there. I had no desire to
muddy the waters, but at the same time, if the fullness of
truth was revealed somewhere, I did not want to stop short
of reaching it. The journey to find Christ had been long and
arduous, and I would not be comfortable until I made sure
to get off at the right stop.

The thought of seeking out a Catholic church in Ankara
did not occur to me right away. I did not want to become
emotionally involved with a parish, by making friends and
getting to know people, before making the decision to become Catholic. But at the same time, my confusion was
unrelenting.

Finally, I decided to talk to a priest, even though I had
never met a priest before, let alone had a deep a conversation with one. How would I find a Catholic church in
the capital of my nation, a city of over four million? Uncle
Google told me that there was one on the grounds of the

Vatican Embassy. But that location did not appeal to me, since it was in the middle of where all the other embassies were. Embassy row did not sound like an inviting or ideal place to seek answers.

Thankfully there was another church. Azize Tereza (Saint Therese) was in the old part of the city on the grounds of the French Embassy. I had a general idea of where it was, but I did not recall seeing anything that resembled a church there. It was better to give them a call and to make an appointment rather than being turned away after traveling across the big city.

With a mixture of reluctance and expectation, I dialed the number to the one and only Catholic church that offered Mass in Turkish. I talked to a very amiable but nevertheless suspicious young lady, who very amiably and suspiciously told me that the priest was busy. *Hmm.*

"Thank you. I'll call back later."

I did call back later, more than once, and the priest was busy again and again. I felt like the widow in Christ's parable who would not stop knocking on the judge's door. Like her, I stubbornly kept trying. On my fifth attempt, the people at the church office and the priest must have had enough, for a man with a thick accent picked up the phone and told me how unusual it was for him to receive such calls. I briefly explained my dilemma between Protestantism and Catholicism and asked if I could bother him with a visit to discuss some questions I had. After having thoroughly questioned me over the phone to check the sincerity and the sanity of the young woman who would not stop pestering his staff, the kind priest agreed to meet me.

As previously mentioned, Christians, especially Catholics and Orthodox, have a very bad reputation in Turkey. In addition, wearing any form of religious garb in public is technically forbidden. This law was passed a little after the foundation of the republic to encourage imams and other Muslim clergy to wear Western clothing. It was also to deter religiously motivated riots. The law, however, extends to people of other faiths, such as Christians and Jews. As a result, the group of Franciscan sisters who worked for the nuncio at the Vatican Embassy traveled only by cab, because they were not allowed to forgo their habits for civilian clothing. Thankfully, their duty did not extend beyond the limits of the embassy, and the only time they needed to travel was to visit the Church of Saint Therese. Of course, the priests who served at Saint Therese needed more freedom, so they wore civilian clothes whenever they left church grounds.

The historical prejudice against Catholics made clergy and laymen alike suspicious of newcomers. Open evangelization was out of the question, because they did not want to attract the wrath of their neighbors, which mostly consisted of conservative Muslim shopkeepers. The situation is somewhat different in Istanbul, which is a more cosmopolitan city, but in Ankara one had to keep his head down in the neighborhood where the Catholic church was located. Making sure that my head was down, I made the ninety-minute trip from my dorm to Saint Therese.

It was a snowy December day on the cold plains of central Anatolia. I did not want to spend that much time outdoors in the freezing temperatures but, alas, the Holy Spirit was insistent. Also, I wanted to get out of the murky waters in which I seemed to be stuck since I started reading Mr. Shea's book. I needed fresh eyes to help me, as the eyes of those around me only rolled with disapproval. One can handle only so much criticism a day, and my quota was met for the year.

Mostly nervous and slightly hopeful, I approached the little building that was marked with the number the priest gave me. It did not look like a church, but it certainly was the right place. The two-story building was painted yellowish beige and sported turquoise shutters. It appeared to have about eight rooms on each floor, if every window corresponded to a room. The small yard was surrounded with high stone walls, and the entrance was barred with equally high cast-iron gates.

I rang the bell.

A man in his late sixties or early seventies wearing a black shirt and black slacks opened the door. He must be the priest, I thought. The building was clearly old but very well kept. Spiral stairs across from the entrance led upstairs and downstairs. The priest, who had a gentle face and a kind smile, led me down stairs to a little community room. A young woman in her early thirties was busy in the nearby kitchen. The priest showed me to the couches in the community room and headed to the kitchen. A few minutes later, he came back with a tray with two teacups filled with hot water. He seemed to be brewing some kind of herbal tea.

The social hierarchy I was raised with made it very uncomfortable for me to talk to a man of his age about anything, let alone something as intimate as my spiritual problems. Having had no close ties with grandparents did not help either. I felt awkward. I sipped the herbal tea to gather my courage. It was fennel.

After he settled on the couch across from me, the old gentleman told me a little bit about himself. Father Patrice was a French Jesuit of seventy-two years, and he had moved to Turkey about a year ago. He had lived in Chad for thirty years before being sent to Ankara. I could not imagine learning a brand new language as difficult as Turkish at his age, but he seemed to have mastered it fairly well, such that we could carry on a conversation. Thankfully, my French was still pretty good; so between Turkish, French, and English we could communicate without any problem. Also, there was a dictionary. Yes, there always was a dictionary.

Father Patrice presented himself as if he were just an old grandfather who liked nothing more than drinking hot chocolate and watching black-and-white movies. His amiable demeanor thawed the icy chill I seemed to be producing. After the introductions, he went on in a monologue about how different the Turkish and the Arabic languages were and about the benefits of fennel tea. At the end of ten minutes, my seat felt much more comfortable, and the room appeared much cozier.

I think I talked for almost half an hour without a break after he asked what brought me to this part of the city on such an awful winter day. I talked and talked until everything that bothered me was on the table. Once all that was said, I finished my cold fennel tea and leaned back in the armchair. I felt a bit lighter, and things that seemed to be such big deals were not as worrisome anymore.

It was not very hard to see how confused I was, especially to someone as experienced in matters of mind and soul as Father Patrice. A warm, understanding smile spread across his wise face, and he said I needed time. Contrary to what I believed, there was no need to make a decision right then or even anytime soon. He suggested that I take a step back and let all the mud settle to the bottom, so that I could see clearly. To help me in the endeavor of settling the mud, he gave me three assignments.

I was to pray, not in the frantic way I had been praying, but in a way that was more open to hearing from the Lord. I did not know what he was talking about, since I was not familiar with contemplative prayer at all. He wrote down some verses for me and asked me to pray, read, pray, listen.

I could do that. There was a lot of listening that I was not used to, but I accepted the challenge. I didn't realize how loud and crowded it was inside my head.

Secondly, I was to paint a picture after this prayer. During our conversation, he asked what I enjoyed doing other than acting frantic. I told him that despite being mostly talentless, I enjoyed drawing and painting. He told me that painting or drawing could be a form of prayer as well. I said I would try.

Lastly, he asked me to come to Mass on Sundays and just be. I was not supposed to try to find a solution or to make a decision. I was to come to Mass, pray with all the people there, and just be.

He knew that I needed to calm down. I was like an over-tired toddler. I wanted to run around in circles until gravity gave way, but all I needed was a good night's rest. I needed a parent to put me to bed with a firm hand. That was who Father Patrice became for me, a parent who had a warm, inviting smile and wise words, who was not afraid of stopping me when I wanted to run.

I do not like running, anyway.

The following few days were intense and calming at the same time. The wise priest had directed me to stop constantly thinking about myself and relying on my own understanding and instead to look upon the crucified Christ. As I read and contemplated the Scriptures and said prayers that involved both talking and listening, the veil through which I had been looking at the world slowly parted. In my quest to find the truth about the Catholic Church, the pressure to find the answers, real or perceived, had taken me away from the foot of the Cross. I found myself being pulled to one specific passage over and over again:

And behold, a woman of the city, who was a sinner, when she learned that he was sitting at table in the Pharisee's house, brought an alabaster flask of ointment, and standing behind him at his feet, weeping, she began to wet his feet with her tears, and wiped them with the hair of her head, and kissed his feet, and anointed them with the ointment. (Lk 7:37–38)

I do not know why this passage kept creeping into my mind, but it once more reminded me who was the Lord and who was the sinner. I had forgotten that I had to be more like the woman in this passage, pouring my riches at his feet and waiting for His answer and His guidance. Like me, this woman had many sins, and she had humbly come before Jesus and given Him all that she had, along with her tears. I painted a picture of the scene as I prayed over this Scripture and wished to be humble and generous like this unnamed woman whom Jesus exalted in front of the Pharisees.

This woman's example also advised me that as long as I knelt before Christ, my heart and mind would eventually calm down so that I could see clearly. I had read and researched to the extent of my ability and resources. My intellect had done its job, but as the saying goes, the distance between the brain and the heart is rather long. The woman who washed Christ's feet with her tears was urging me to put my pride aside and to follow where my reason was leading me.

~

The following Sunday, I woke up early again to take the bus to the city for morning Mass. (When I say early, I mean earlier than all my friends, not early like my toddler, who is awake at five in the morning. One's perspective changes over time.) I had been to Mass once before, at Anthony's request, in Istanbul, but that was when I had no intention of becoming Catholic. Actually, the first time I visited that historical church, Saint Anthony's (in Turkish Sen Antuan), I remember looking up at the giant crucifix and being displeased with it. I told the friend who was with me that I did not understand the Catholic obsession with the Crucifixion since, because of the Resurrection, the cross was now empty. Ah, my reaction only showed how much I was unable to grasp the depth of either. I also had little comprehension of the Eucharist. So, when I went to Mass at Sen Antuan the previous year, it was more as a tourist than as a pilgrim.

This wintry Sunday in Ankara was much different. Having done the assignments that Father Patrice recommended, I felt a little more at peace. He was right to suggest that before I took a step, I should calm the storm and clear the water. In the midst of the turmoil I put myself through, I lacked vision and clarity. Prayer and contemplation had already started to bring some much needed serenity to my mind and soul.

As I entered the front yard of the building that did not look like a church, instead of the quiet of my previous weekday visit, I was greeted by parked cars along the sidewalk and the chatter of a handful of people walking to the church. It was comforting to know that there would be a crowd I could blend into.

When in doubt one is always tempted to follow the crowd to find the way out, or in, in this case. Since I had seen only the basement floor of the beige building, I had no clue about where Mass would take place. Instead of going down, the small crowd followed the cast-iron spiral stairs to the top floor. Through an entrance no bigger than two front doors put together, we entered a chapel that should not have been there. I felt as though I had traveled inside TARDIS, the time machine in *Doctor Who*, and had entered a different dimension. The eight windows I had seen from the outside proved to be hiding and protecting beautiful stained-glass windows decorating the chapel walls. It was slightly magical. I felt as if we were hidden from the world.

I found an inconspicuous spot in the back and settled in one of the wooden pews. From there I could observe everything that was happening in the sanctuary yet remain as invisible as possible. A small part of me was hoping to observe something utterly objectionable so that I could put this confusing chapter behind me and move on with my merry Protestant life. That little part of me was deeply disappointed.

The Mass was reverent and beautiful. One of the things I could not get used to in the Evangelical churches I attended was the style of worship. Neither in nondenominational nor in charismatic congregations did I feel as though we were standing in the presence of God or kneeling in adoration before Him. I felt rather as though we were hanging out with our pal Jesus.

If we actually believe that we are the sons and daughters of the almighty God, who created the endless cosmos and the tiniest cells in our bodies, I thought we should fall on our knees often or at least once a week on Sundays. I loved that during the Eucharistic prayer, every man and woman knelt in silent reverence. It was clear that there was something significant and awe-inspiring taking place. This was a Lord I would not hesitate to follow, because He had humbled Himself to be my friend, even though He had created the heavens and the earth.

Another surprising and attractive aspect of Mass was the

infusion of the Holy Scriptures in every aspect, prayer, and greeting. I do not know why this was so surprising to me, since it was the Catholic Church who gave us the Bible, but it is hard to get rid of prejudices in a matter of months. I was expecting to hear made-up objectionable lines at every turn. Instead, I found myself recognizing lines from the Gospels and the epistles.

This was also the first time I sincerely started to question whether I believed in the Real Presence. To be honest, I did not have much trouble accepting that Christ actually meant what He said about eating His flesh and drinking His blood. It had never made sense to me that He could have been talking figuratively, since so many left Him, finding His words impossible to accept. The early Christians, whom many Protestants strive to imitate, did not seem to take Jesus' words figuratively either. The scriptural and historical evidence was clear to me, but believing that each and every priest performed a miracle during each and every Mass was a little harder to swallow.

It appeared that the people in the congregation did not share my doubt, as there was an atmosphere of awe from the beginning of the "Holy, Holy, Holy" to the end of Mass. Everyone slowly and reverently approached the altar to receive the Body of Christ. Touching the Divine Body was reserved for the priest; the people folded their hands and opened their mouths to receive the spiritual manna. I remained on my seat as a doubting but impressed observer.

Ignorant though I was, it was obvious that one could not become Catholic unless he believed in the Real Presence. Everything in the Mass led to the Consecration and the consumption of the Divine Host. The climax of the Mass is not the singing, the readings, or the homily. The paramount goal is to equip the people of God with the ultimate source of their strength, the Eucharist, so that when they go out into the world, they can live and preach the gospel. I was rather happy with the three-point Jesuit homily, which was thankfully much shorter than the typical Sunday sermons I had heard, and it was clear to me that the Scripture readings, the homily, and the prayers all served to prepare the mind and the soul for union with God.

It was profound.

If the Eucharist was indeed the Flesh and Blood of Christ, then by not receiving this wonderful gift regularly, I was a bird that had clipped its own wings. As a Protestant, I strove to live a holy life, and I knew many other Protestants who lived truly remarkable and admirable lives. Yet, without the Eucharist we were still only walking, when with the Eucharist we could be flying.

Although the Bible was clear that Christ Himself instituted the Eucharist (Jn 6:51, 53–55; 1 Cor 11:23–25), I admitted to myself that I did not yet believe in the Real Presence. As a result, I really did not belong at that Mass. After the final blessing, as the faithful said, "Thanks be to God", I tried to get away without being noticed, but let's face it, there are not many people at a Catholic Mass in Ankara. Unless one has the skill to blend into the background or become invisible on demand, one must endure a few introductions.

Since there was only one exit, I could not escape the priest. The windows were not very conducive to a timely escape for potential doubters. Architects can be very thoughtless. Even though I feared a conversation with the grandfatherly priest and expected some sort of scolding as if I were still a little girl, Father Patrice only asked me whether there was any time in my schedule to meet him during the upcoming week. Since he did not seem to be hitting me on the head with the *Catechism* or the Bible (I would hate to damage the book with my big, hard head), I agreed to see him again and talk a little more about the Eucharist.

Before our meeting I wanted to become a little more informed about transubstantiation and some other big words Catholics have devised to explain complicated mysteries. Although it was very hard to believe in daily miracles, I was willing to give the Catholic Church the benefit of the doubt, because, after all, she had gotten many other things right. I set out to see what my trusty laptop had to offer in regard to explaining the Eucharist. I could not thank enough the man who invented the internet. Libraries in Muslim countries do not offer much on Catholic teaching.

On the internet I came across a list of descriptions of various eucharistic miracles. As it has been established in this memoir, I am not easily convinced of miracles, but since the topic piqued my interest at that moment, I started to read about the many accounts of these miracles.

Thankfully, I was not the only doubter. Throughout the centuries, many religious have lost faith in the Real Presence, and in His infinite mercy and patience, the Lord performed some very convincing miracles that have been approved by the Church. If you are familiar with the canonization process, you know that the Catholic Church does not take claims of miracles and apparitions lightly. For a phenomenon to be declared a miracle, a board of doctors and scientists, not necessarily Catholic, must rule that the phenomenon cannot be explained by scientific measures. The number of miracles attributed to the Real Presence exceeds one hundred, but I remember reading about two in particular that sent chills down my spine in my little dorm room.

The first eucharistic miracle that made me shudder was one of the earliest recorded miracles. The Desert Fathers recorded that one of the monks had harbored doubts about the Real Presence. Troubled by this, the other monks prayed that the faith of their fellow monk would be restored. During a Mass they attended together, these men, including the doubting monk, saw a child on the altar as the bread was placed there. According to their accounts, as the priest started to break the bread, an angel descended with a sword and poured the child's blood into the chalice. As the priest broke the bread into pieces, the angel cut the child into pieces. As people approached the altar to receive the Eucharist, only the doubting monk received a morsel of flesh covered in blood. He became scared and prayed: "Lord, I believe that this bread is your flesh and this chalice your blood." The bloody flesh then became bread, and with a thankful heart the monk received it.[1]

Having studied history for some time by that point, I knew that the accounts of the monks were trustworthy. Even in my department, which was quite secular by any account, historians relied on the chronicles and documents of the Catholic Church. This was because monks of the past who recorded events, deaths, births, and baptisms were nothing if not scrupulous. Actually, I had always wondered why historians almost always trusted the documents of the Catholic Church except when they talked about miracles. If they were reliable in recording historical events and weddings, why would they not be truthful about spiritual matters? If the monks were so fastidious that even wrongdoings by members of the Church, including popes and priests, were documented, why would they suddenly all go God-crazy and make up stories about apparitions and bloody transformations?

[1] Roy Rychlak, "Eucharistic Miracles: Evidence of the Real Presence", *Catholic Answers Magazine*, February 2, 2016, https://www.catholic.com/magazine/print-edition/eucharistic-miracles-evidence-of-the-real-presence-0.

What was most enlightening for me in this Desert Father's miracle was how visually descriptive Christ's sacrifice was. His childlike innocence and the undeserved torture He endured on our behalf were illuminated so vividly. It shed light on why Catholics remained so somber during the Consecration.

The other eucharistic miracle that stayed with me took place in the thirteenth century. Peter of Prague was a German priest who traveled to Rome on a pilgrimage. Even though by all accounts he was considered a pious priest, he had doubts about the Real Presence. He celebrated Mass in a church above the tomb of Saint Christina, and as soon as he said the words of Consecration, blood started to trickle from the Host and over his hands and onto the altar.

He was confused at first and tried to hide the blood, but after realizing what was happening, he asked to be taken to Pope Urban IV. The pope listened to the priest and sent investigators to find out the truth of the matter. When it became apparent that the priest's account was factual, Pope Urban ordered the Host and the bloodstained cloths to be brought to Orvieto, where he resided.

After this encounter, it is said that the pope asked Thomas Aquinas to compose the Proper for a Mass honoring the Holy Eucharist as the Body of Christ. The year following the miracle, Pope Urban instituted the feast of Corpus Christi.[2]

This time it was a priest who had doubts. This priest had been ordained by a bishop so that he could perform this rite, yet he doubted its efficacy, even as he went on a pilgrim-

---

[2] Joan Carroll Cruz, *Eucharistic Miracles* (Charlotte, N.C.: TAN Books, 1987), quoted in "Eucharistic Miracle, Bolsena-Orvieto, Italy", Real Presence Eucharistic Education and Adoration Association, http://www.therealpr esence.org/eucharst/mir/bolsena.html.

age. Despite his doubt, the bread became the flesh of Christ as he said the words, because the priest's current disposition was irrelevant. Christ had made a promise, and Christ would keep it. I imagined this man of God being tortured by the doubt he carried into every Mass he celebrated. He was not a mere college student who was trying to figure out whether the Catholic Church was the one true church. His life revolved around the very altar whose usefulness he doubted. As I pictured this godly man's spiritual dilemma, a wave of gladness and gratitude came over me. I was glad and grateful because I was not the only one who carried around a skeptical heart and mind, and because our God is willing to put up with our doubtful hearts and let us touch His wounds, unlike Allah, who would strike down the one who carried even a seed of doubt.

The intellectual acceptance of the Real Presence had started to travel to my heart. "Faith is what someone knows to be true, whether they believe it or not",[3] said Flannery O'Connor, and finally I had started to believe. Reading the myriad of accounts of eucharistic miracles left me amazed at the prospect of partaking in a miracle every Sunday. It made sense that there was kneeling and hushed reverence in the Catholic Mass. If the crucified Christ was a part of the Christian life in a real miraculous sense, there was no place else to be.

[3] Flannery O'Connor, *Wise Blood* (New York: Farrar, Straus and Giroux, 2007).

18

Traveling to Rome via England

I do not know when exactly I made the decision to become Catholic, but the night I read the unexplainable accounts of bloodstained cloths, weeping statues, and angels descending was definitely a turning point. When I woke up the following morning, the nagging hesitation and the desire to blend into the wall of Saint Therese Church was gone. I looked forward to my next meeting with Father Patrice.

From then on, becoming a part of the tiny parish of Saint Therese came naturally. I didn't mind making the hour-and-a-half commute to the little chapel for a simple meal with the Franciscan nuns who spoke neither Turkish nor English; or for a study of the Gospel of Matthew with Father and a few other young faithful souls. The beige building that didn't look as if it belonged to that part of the town became a regular destination.

Weekly Mass attendance grew the little seed of wonder that was planted by the faithful recordings of the doubters before me. The quiet, prayerful stretches during Mass and the unfamiliar smell of the incense became rare occasions I looked forward to during the week. Since the priest wanted to make sure that our desire to be confirmed was not fleeting, those who expressed interest in becoming Catholic did

169

not quite know when we would walk up the aisle to receive Communion. Because of the absence of regular converts, there was not an established Rite of Christian Initiation of Adults (RCIA) program, so we received our religious instruction through Scripture studies and spaghetti dinners. It was such a small and intimate group that we all became close friends in a short time.

It was my last year at Bilkent University, and I had decided what to do when I received my master's degree. Since teaching and being around college students had become a passion, I would get a doctorate; then the life of an academic awaited me. I had applied to Bilkent and three universities in England. I did not want to go any farther than England, so I had no desire to study in the United States. I really didn't think it would be possible for me to get a doctorate in England either, because I simply did not have the financial means to do so. I applied more as an excuse to check the box that said "applied abroad and rejected".

To my surprise, Durham University sent me a letter informing me that their Politics Department had no qualms about letting me study there. But since money does not grow on trees, I figured there was no way I would be able to pay the thirty thousand pounds per year needed for my studies. The Turkish government is not as obliging as that of the United States in paying tuition fees in the form of guaranteed student loans. They like to keep things simple: You pay the government, the government does not pay you. So I bragged about the acceptance letter and then went to tell the Political Science Department at Bilkent that I would be delighted to be part of their graduate team.

The summer of 2007 was almost over when I received another letter from Durham University. This time the sweet words informed me that the department had awarded me a scholarship, which would cover my tuition fees and offer a small stipend. It would not be enough for me to live in England, but the major cost was taken care of. It was sudden and unexpected, because I had not applied for a scholarship. As if I had won the lottery that I had never entered, suspicions about the authenticity of the letter prompted me to talk to a person from the department. I was assured that it was not a scheme. Durham is one of the best universities in Europe, and a higher degree from there would open the door to any university in Turkey. It was unquestionably a wonderful opportunity.

It was August already, and the university expected me to arrive in Durham at the end of September. That was not much time to move to a different country. Frantically, I talked to my friends who had been to or studied in England, and I was satisfied that this adventure would be a worthy undertaking. As I started to get the papers ready for the painful visa process, friends and some family helped me to put a little fund together until such a time as I got settled in my new country and found a job. The months of August and September melted away, and I found myself at the Ankara airport being sent off by my father and Bora.

It was all surreal.

~

I flew to London and took a train from Kings Cross Station to Durham for the last, three-hour leg of my journey from Ankara. I had read up on the British Isles and had looked at pictures online, so I had some idea of what to expect, but mere words and pictures cannot prepare a person for the experience of moving to another country all by oneself and without any support to speak of. As in Shakespeare's *Tempest*, I had landed in a brave new world.

As the train traveled through northern England, I couldn't help admiring the small towns, the rows of brick houses, and the rolling green hills. Everything was so different from Turkey that I wondered if I had stepped through a looking glass into a Jane Austen story set in the English countryside. As I stared out the window, the Durham Cathedral suddenly filled my view with all its glory. The seat of the bishop of Durham was built a thousand years ago and is considered one of the finest examples of Norman architecture. It was simply breathtaking.

Everything about England was strange. I had been to America, Germany, and Belgium, but I had visited those places with friends or had someone to meet me at the airport. Here, in this magical land of gray and green, the almost empty train station seemed eager to welcome this newcomer. I took a cab to the university and hauled my one suitcase containing my belongings to the dorm room.

Durham was a small city that grew around the cathedral and the River Wear. The curving, deep, dark river formed a peninsula where the cathedral, the castle, and the city center were located. Here also were the university's older buildings and Saint Cuthbert's Catholic Church. The rest of the town and the modern buildings rose mostly on the other side of the river. Having had the happy misfortune of seeing Durham first, it was hard to be as impressed by any other English city. Even London cannot capture the quaint Tolkienesque feeling of Durham.

After settling in for a few days and exploring the wonderful landscape along the river, I met the young priest of Saint Cuthbert's. Father Tony was in his thirties and seemed to enjoy being the pastor of the university parish. He listened to my story and informed me about the RCIA program. Unlike in Turkey, there were many who wished to be confirmed at the upcoming Easter Vigil.

About ten of us from the university joined the RCIA program. I was one of the older candidates. At twenty-seven I was considered a mature student, regardless of my maturity level. It was not politically correct to call us old or get-a-job-already perpetual students. The British are thoughtful like that. We met every Wednesday evening to go through the material. I was already familiar with most of the information, because of my previous research and my time spent at Saint Therese. It was technically my second RCIA, and all I wanted was to finish the class quickly and to be received into full communion with the Catholic Church. Father Patrice had told me that it would be better to enter the Church at Saint Cuthbert's because it would be my parish for a while afterward.

The months passed in England at a much slower and less remarkable rate than I had expected, although I enjoyed the scenery and the constant tea drinking. When my funds had dwindled, I started to look for a job, and after a couple of months, I got a paid position in Newcastle upon Tyne as a refugee support person for the Catholic diocese there. Another help was working as a volunteer with people with learning disabilities. Since this job required that I live close to those I served, it came with an apartment. The refugee-support job provided enough money to cover my reduced costs, so I was content and thankful.

I continued to attend RCIA classes, and the following months went by fast. Before I knew it, Ash Wednesday of 2008 was upon me. At the end of this penitential season of Lent, I would finally receive the Body of Christ. Every little Lenten sacrifice I made was more meaningful, and every daily Mass I attended drew me closer to God. It pained me to sit patiently while everyone else approached the altar, but the end of my waiting was near.

The British students and most of the international students were gone for Easter break. Thus, Durham was quieter than usual during Holy Week. Father Tony invited the students who remained over the holiday to reside in the rectory, which hosted a few students or visitors throughout the year. That way we could all pray the Liturgy of the Hours together and be better prepared for the upcoming Easter.

As Holy Week came to an end, there remained the heavy prospect of another sacrament. One of the crucial preparations for confirmation is confession. Father Tony had asked a few other priests to hear confessions during one of the Fridays of Lent. Of course, I was not looking forward to spilling my sins in front of a stranger, least of all an English priest. The British accent always made me think I was about to be corrected for something I had done wrong. With the dread of talking about my sins added to this, I had become very nervous and reluctant about confession. Of course, looking forward to talking about my sins would certainly have been odd, so I suppose my reaction to the coming ordeal was only natural.

I had researched how to make a good confession and memorized almost all the prayers, except for the Act of Contrition. (I am still working on it.) As I walked up the hill to Saint Cuthbert's, something other than my lack of enthusiasm for confession made my heart heavy. I did not exactly know what was troubling me. I entered the church through the heavy wooden doors, and someone directed me to the priest who was sitting in one of the reconciliation rooms. A leather chair was positioned across from him. I would have preferred a screen and a kneeler for anonymity, but one cannot have it all.

He was a middle-aged priest with the air of one who had heard many confessions and had accumulated knowledge and wisdom beyond his years. Quickly I summarized my history, emphasizing that it was my first confession. He asked "Why are you here?" I answered, "Because I need the sacrament of reconciliation before the sacrament of confirmation." *Are you not aware of the inner workings of the Catholic Church? Geesh.*

He asked again, "No, why are *you* here?" I realized that he was asking a deeper question. I paused a moment, but only a moment, because my soul knew what was burdening me. The answer came without hesitation: "I killed my own babies." Everything I did before my baptism was cleansed as the baptismal waters washed over me. I knew that. He knew that. However, there is power in the words that are spoken by the one acting in the person of Christ. I needed to hear the words of absolution, just like the sinful woman who washed Jesus' feet with her tears.

This wise priest whose name I do not remember and whom I never saw again told me, just as his Savior had told many before him, that my sins were forgiven. That was when I fully grasped the importance and the power of confession. It was so much better to talk to a flesh-and-blood person about my transgressions than to kneel next to my bed and talk to the ceiling. In addition to having my sins absolved, I experienced the benefit of admitting that I was selfish, weak, and rebellious. Such truth telling is an added incentive to avoid sin. I wanted to please the Lord and to avoid spending eternity in hell. But we are physical beings, and the desire to please God and to avoid damnation is not always sufficient to overcome the temptations of the world, the flesh, and the devil. There have been many sins that I have come very close to committing but steered clear of because I simply hated the thought of having to bring them to the confessional.

I left the church a changed person. If I were to die in an accident, that would have been a good time. Thankfully, cars went by without hitting me, even though I still was not used to the drive-on-the-left rule.

The day after that very good Good Friday, I joined several others as the priest anointed us with blessed oil and informed us that we were finally in full communion with the Church that was founded by Christ. Now, just like millions of other brothers and sisters, I could receive the Body of Christ. It was wonderful, humbling, and freeing all at the same time to become a part of something bigger than myself. It was wonderful to trust that Christ would guide me and keep me on the right path. I did not have to decide for myself what was right and what was wrong. I walked back to my pew with a renewed and lightened spirit.

From then on, many articles, documents, and books about Catholicism passed through my hands. Learning about the faith is like scuba diving, I imagined. I cannot scuba dive, but I know that the ocean is not limited to what one sees on the surface. The endless colored reefs inhabited by artfully painted fish can be seen only by diving down. Being a Protestant, I was in the ocean, but I was swimming on the surface, ignorant of the riches that awaited me in the depths. The more I read, the more fascinating and rich the millennia-old Church became. I was captivated by the wonder of learning how different doctrines came to be, how Mary was the new Ark of the Covenant, how much Saint

Thomas wrote, and that people thousands of years ago said similar words during Mass.

Slowly the Catholic Church became the home I never knew I had lost. Daily Mass and the Liturgy of the Hours were comforts during the short, dark days of the English north. Stopping by the café next to the cathedral to enjoy a cup of tea and a blueberry scone while reading a book from the Catholic bookstore next door became part of my routine. I was at peace spiritually for the first time in years.

19

Finding My Better Half
across the Atlantic

The year 2009 rolled in quickly, but my dissertation was coming along slowly and painfully. With the solitude that came with being a single doctoral student I read the Harry Potter series and various Terry Pratchett books and caught up on missed *Doctor Who* episodes. Needless to say, I needed to find my vocation.

Being single was hard, but it had been my state of life for quite some time. Thinking about being single for the rest of my life was not necessarily depressing, but it certainly was not appealing either. As my thirties stretched before me, only the thought of growing old alone seemed to bother me. I had not given much consideration to having children, because I had made a decision a few years before not to romanticize married life so as not to make my current state harder to bear. I did not watch romantic dramas or comedies, and I did not dwell on having a baby or a family. I tried to be as open as possible to whatever route the Lord wanted me to travel.

At the same time, having to live a mostly solitary life with only a handful of friends made me realize that my chances of finding a husband who took his faith as seriously as I did was getting slimmer by the year. Since communities didn't have dances or social gatherings anymore, I was, in a way, stuck. My family and friends in Turkey were getting concerned about my becoming a spinster. Nobody in their right mind would marry me after I turned thirty, they thought. It was hard enough to find someone when I was young and beautiful, but after thirty, all bets were off.

With countless hours of nagging and not-so-subtle hint dropping from my family and friends piled on top of my own worries about aging alone, I decided to give online dating a try, as a few of my friends suggested. To be honest, I was not hopeful at all, even though I had read and heard that more and more marriages were happening through online sites. Though these marriages proved to be among the more stable ones, I remained skeptical, as my personality demanded.

For me, only a Catholic site would do. My faith had become such an integral part of my life that the thought of spending the rest of my days with someone who did not share the same views or even the same enthusiasm was unimaginable. I would rather have stayed single. This train of thought took me to CatholicMatch.com. My bank account would not allow me to be a long-term member, but there was enough for me to sign up for three months and see if this whole endeavor was worth the effort.

I signed up and filled out the forms asking for my hair color, my interests, and whether I had tattoos. After some consideration, I decided to use my confirmation name, Irene, instead of my obviously Turkish and painful-to-pronounce first name.

One of the sections of a person's profile on this website asks if one agrees with the Church's teachings in several important areas. The question of why anyone would want to remain Catholic if he did not agree with the Church was rather confusing to this fairly new Catholic. I checked all the boxes to indicate that I agreed with the Church about crucial matters, such as the Eucharist, contraception, the sanctity of life, papal infallibility, premarital sex, the Immaculate Conception, and holy orders.

After making sure that my search parameters included only men who also affirmed Church teaching, I looked around a bit. I clicked on a few profiles. Nobody really jumped out at me, and I did not hear a voice telling me which of these tiny photographs depicted the face of the man I would spend my life with. I sighed and signed off.

Oh well, I had three months; maybe someone would turn up. If not, I could at least tell myself and my nosy but well-meaning friends that I had tried.

Life got in the way, and the website remained forgotten for a couple of weeks. When I signed on to see if anyone promising had popped up, I found that several people were interested in me. I looked through the profiles to see, first of all, if they and I were on the same page regarding the faith. Some were; some were not. I proceeded to read the notes from those who seemed to be more serious about being Catholic. Nothing stood out. I sighed as I scrolled down, thinking about ending this exercise in futility.

Right before I signed out, a short recent message caught my attention. An American living thousands of miles away had asked whether I wanted to go out for fish and chips. That was all there was in his message. I looked at his profile, and even though there were no lightning bolts, he seemed like someone I could possibly connect with, most of all because he had converted to Catholicism at about the same age as I was when I converted to Christianity.

Virgil was the first man I talked with on that website, so I didn't know what to expect. He had already gone out with a few girls he met through CatholicMatch, so thankfully at least one of us was a little experienced. Even though he told me that he was in the U.S. Air Force and currently stationed in San Antonio, Texas, I was sure that he was a serial killer who preyed on unsuspecting young women. *Ha! He would not find me an easy prey!* On second thought, I didn't quite know why he would go through the trouble of finding a victim who required air travel and was thus bound to increase the paper trail and the incriminating evidence, but who knew what went through a serial killer's mind?

As we exchanged messages through the website, I sought to verify that the stuff he said checked out. Was there really an Air Force base where he said there was? Why did he write me so early in the day? I had no idea what time the American military would expect a person to wake up, but surely it wasn't 6 A.M. I was mistaken. He woke up even earlier. Excuse my civilian ignorance.

After a week or so, I was almost convinced that the insightful and humorous e-mails that showed up in my inbox every day were not written by a serial killer. What a relief!

Virgil was smart, witty, and charming. When I woke up in the morning, I loved making myself a cup of tea to accompany my breakfast crumpets and settling down to read his long e-mail. Our correspondence made every day a little more joyful and the rainy English spring a little more bearable. Each e-mail we sent each other was pages long, which possibly took at least an hour to type, if not longer. We were getting to know each other in the virtual world well before the real one.

Even before the amazing invention of Skype built a thousand-mile bridge between us, Virgil and I, on the white pages of a computer screen, talked about how we became Christians, how we were brought up, how we wanted to raise children, whether we ate meat on Fridays, and whether I could ever learn to enjoy baseball or eat Tabasco sauce. Without the complications of physical attraction and the anxiety of trying to impress the opposite sex, it was wonderful and almost stress-free to make sure that the relationship would not be a fleeting romance, but a lifelong commitment. If either of us was not happy with the other's beliefs or outlook on life, it would be much easier to call it a day and sign off.

By the end of the first six weeks, we had comfortably established that our beliefs and goals in life were very similar. I believed that he would strive to lead me and our very possible future children to heaven. I respected him, and I had a suspicion that I was in love with him. It was a little hard, however, to establish that everything would work out just on a computer screen. Neither of us was willing to take the relationship any further without making sure that we found each other attractive. One might think that we were shallow, but after all, it would be unrealistic for us physical beings to expect that the marriage would be a success without at least some mutual physical attraction.

We had talked about everything we cared about. He was thirty-four, and I was twenty-nine. We knew that even if we talked another year, there wouldn't be much to uncover that might change our lives. The next step was to ditch the computer and to meet in the fragile world of flesh and blood.

At the beginning of May, less than two months from the first time Virgil asked me to have fish and chips, the decision to meet was already made; only the logistics were left to plan.

He couldn't take time off until August, but I was free to take time off as long as my employer was informed two weeks in advance. I sacrificed the time Virgil didn't have and he sacrificed the money I didn't have. I was America-bound again, but this time to find out whether the man I would spend my life with might be waiting at the other end of the trans-Atlantic flight.

Naturally, the thought occurred to me that, regardless of my age, I was acting like a teenager. I have been known to do stupid things, possibly many more than a sensible person should admit. Was I about to make yet another lamentable mistake? It did not help that I was still terrified of getting married, despite the fact that the thought of growing old alone alleviated some of my commitment issues. Dr. Ray would not approve my using the word "issues", but there was a possibility of commitment and my very complicated approach to it, so "issues" it is.

In order to bring some sort of sanity to what appeared to be a lunatic affair, I decided to contact Raymond and Agnes, who now resided in Texas, not far from where Virgil was stationed. I reasoned that, if after Virgil and I spent the day with them, these people who had known me for a long time and whom I considered to be very wise approved this man as marriage material, my anxieties and fears would dissipate. Getting the approval of people I deeply respected would also assure me that I was not acting like a teenager.

During the long flight over the Atlantic Ocean, I kept thinking that I had lost all common sense and kept asking myself why they did not serve alcohol for free anymore. I kept replaying the e-mails, the letters, and the hours-long conversations in my head just to make sure that I was not on a fool's errand. At the same, while waiting for me, Virgil was possibly wondering if he had wasted his hard-earned money on some silly Turkish girl.

In New York, the usual unpleasantries of going through

customs and visa checkpoints flew by, and I boarded the plane that would take me to Texas. The exhaustion of not having slept for almost a day and the angst of finding out where this adventure would take me resulted in fitful but still much-needed sleep. By the time we landed in San Antonio, my hair was stiff and greasy from the hours of being pressed against the tiny airplane window, and my clothes smelled unsurprisingly as if they had been lived in for two days. The first impression was not going to be as magical as I thought it would be. I spent some time in the bathroom, trying to restore some sanity to my hair, before walking the long corridor at the end of which Virgil would be waiting.

"I must be completely out of my mind," I thought. If my own daughter were to do something like this (are you reading this, Monica?), I would lock her in the basement until she turned gray. I stopped halfway and seriously considered turning back, but I couldn't imagine spending another day on uncomfortable airplane seats and airport benches without a good night's sleep. Also, even though nervousness threatened to overtake my reason, I really wanted to meet this man who had managed to charm me into traveling five thousand miles in a matter of weeks. I kept walking.

I approached the magically opening sliding doors. The first person I saw was Virgil. He was wearing a light-pink polo shirt, jeans, and a blue Detroit Lions hat. He had decided that the Lions needed a fan after having a no-win season, even though he did not watch much football back then. He broke into the kind of gentle smile that one would not expect from a man of his 6-foot-2-inch, 250-pound build. I was relieved to find out that he wasn't a serial killer, since there was no way I would be able to outrun this muscular former Marine who didn't care about wearing pink or being the fan of a losing team.

His friendly manner warmed my heart and eased the tension I had been feeling for the last hour. He was even handsomer than I had expected. Even though we had seen each other on video chats, I could not be sure that we would like each other's appearances. I had tried to picture how tall he was. Many a time a random stranger unknowingly walking the streets of Newcastle had been startled by a Turkish girl trying to walk next to him. I am ashamed to admit that I was that Turkish girl and that I was trying to gauge whether it would be too weird to be next to a man much taller than I.

It wasn't. He was perfect.

I slowly walked toward the exit he was standing near and stopped right in front him. He tossed aside the *Wall Street Journal* in his hands, took a step toward me, and cupped my face in his big hands. After looking into my eyes for a moment, the first words that came out of his mouth were "Can I kiss you?" Looking into his warm green eyes, I nodded.

Then I knew that I was in love with him.

~

I unconsciously touched my engagement ring, as Virgil strove to get comfortable in the tiny seat with less-than-generous foot space. The Boeing passenger jet was taking us to Istanbul, and then to Ankara for our wedding. At times, I still had a hard time believing that the man sitting next to me was unknown to me a year ago and would be my husband in a matter of days.

My visit to the States to meet the man whom Catholic-Match had brought into my life went wonderfully. Raymond and Agnes really liked him, and Virgil passed the day-long test with flying colors, declaring to Raymond that his intention was to marry me. Virgil treated everyone he encountered with utmost kindness and respect; he left hefty tips every time we ate out. The more I watched him interact with others, the more convinced I became that he would make a wonderful husband. The night before I returned to England, he asked me to marry him, producing the ring that now adorned my left hand. I did not have a single ounce of hesitation when I said yes.

My parents had not met Virgil yet, so we decided to get married in Turkey in the church whose gates I had searched for on that snowy winter day to find out whether Catholics might actually be right.

When I told my mother that I was marrying an American, she said she knew that I would end up with a foreigner. Did she say that because I was a Christian or because I was living in England. Who knows? I was glad that she did not make a big deal out of it, even though I knew that my maternal uncles would be less than happy to hear that I would marry an infidel. The first question my father asked after hearing about my engagement was whether Virgil was circumcised. He did not inquire about his job or his financial situation. He did not scold me about the short engagement. He did not even try to say his name properly. Clearly, as long as he was circumcised, everything else would magically sort itself out. I could not help but try to imagine how on earth my five-foot-three-inch father would hold down my soon-to-be husband to have him circumcised. Thankfully, all of us were spared from the realization of that scenario.

A small wedding with my close friends and family was all we wanted. Virgil's mom and his best man, Jeremy, flew from America to witness our joining our lives together. We promised to love and cherish each other until death do us part in front of God, the priest who had gently led me to my home, and the friends who were gracious enough to share our joy.

We knelt before the altar from which we received the Body of Christ for the first time as husband and wife.

I could not have been happier.

20

Coming to America

Having lived in England for two years and having met people from many countries and cultures helped to prepare me for my next move, to a small town in Pennsylvania, which took me even farther away from anything I had known before. Here I encountered wide-open spaces, houses in the middle of nowhere, and endless aisles of breakfast cereal. I experienced both a new freedom and a new aloneness. It was culture shock, pure and simple.

Even though having lived in England helped with my adjustment to America, being confined to our small and peaceful but nevertheless boring town was hard. Therefore, the most pressing issue for me was not learning to drive. Rather, my husband needed to walk me regularly, or I would start eating the furniture.

Unfortunately, I could not apply for a driver's permit without a social security number. I could not get a social security number without a green card, which gives the bearer the status of a permanent resident. We had started the immigration process a while ago, but bureaucracy moves slowly. I had to fill out countless pages of forms, go through health checks that our insurance did not pay for, and spend almost three thousand dollars before the Department of Homeland

Security (DHS) decided that it was all right for me to stay in the United States. All this rigmarole—yet my husband was in the Air Force with a security clearance.

Since people enter into fraudulent marriages to gain entry to the United States, we were required to provide documents such as photographs, plane tickets, and shared credit cards to authenticate our marriage. Also, we were interviewed as a couple. All this was standard procedure, and we were willing to comply with whatever DHS required of us. Our one and only interview did not start as smoothly as I had hoped, however. When we arrived at the gray-walled immigration office that looked more sterile and much less personable than a doctor's office, there were many couples who looked nervous. Virgil did not share their anxiety, as we had done everything that was asked and provided every single document and proof. But part of me was still slightly anxious, because I knew that, despite all our work, an officer who was having a rough day could ruin everything. So we waited. Virgil does not like waiting, because apparently, when he was in the Marines he had to "hurry up and wait" a lot.

After having waited for four hours, Virgil came very close to punching one of the immigration officers when he learned that they had forgotten about us. Thankfully, the not-so-nice officer was not the one who interviewed us. Instead, a lady with a troubled son asked us questions about our marriage for ten minutes and then shared her endless woes with Virgil. My husband's ability to connect with anyone always amazes me.

Soon after the interview, I received the green card, which granted me conditional permanent residence, and then the social security number. The conditions were removed a few years later without an interview when they found out we had a baby together. Really, no fraudulent marriage goes that far. So, I became a legal immigrant who can do anything an American citizen can, except vote. I could work, drive, and pay taxes—nothing like taxation without representation. Later, after another seven hundred dollars, I would be able to become a citizen.

The next hurdle after getting my social security number was to get my driver's license. At the age of thirty-one, I went to the Department of Motor Vehicles for the first time, along with a few sixteen-year-olds. Did I mention that I was seven months pregnant? I aced the written part of the driver's exam. My years of taking tests had made me an expert on multiple-choice questions, but not on driving a machine that required me to use my hands and feet while being alert. Hence, I failed the first driving test without even leaving the parking lot, because even though I could parallel park, I had no idea where my hazard lights were. I failed again the following week. The third time was a charm. At last, my husband didn't need to drive his hysterical pregnant wife to town every time we ran out of milk.

Still, I struggled with making friends, especially after the babies came. The American way of life revolves around individualism, and that is one of the things that makes this country unique. But at the same time, individualism can result in loneliness, especially for a foreigner.

Most of the Eastern cultures value community and family, so much so that often a person's rank or place in society becomes his identity. After all the years of pushing against this close-knit community structure, I have come to the conclusion that a healthy social life contributes immensely to human sanity and happiness.

The isolation and loneliness that result from individualism and urbanism are often too hard to endure for many who move to the United States. It is natural to seek out others like oneself, who are more likely to be from the same country or at least the same religion. The American way of life would have alienated me, too, if it weren't for my Catholic faith, my marriage, and my previously untethered background. America became the place where I lowered my anchor after having drifted aimlessly for so long. Yet I appreciate how hard it is for Muslims, even atheistic ones, to call America home.

~

The Janissary Band of the Ottoman Army was formed to instill fear in the hearts of its enemies. To this day, every Turk who hears the sound of that marching music is filled with reverence, awe, and a little bit of that intimidation their enemies felt centuries ago. That sound harkens to the glorious days of the Ottoman Empire and makes, or should make, today's Christian ask: How was it that Europe was able to stand against the army whose mere band struck terror? How is it that Western civilization seems to be crumbling under the Islamist threat?

The inner peace that comes from being a slave of Allah is important to Islam, and every Muslim is encouraged to attain it. But the outer struggle will not end until all the enemies of Islam are vanquished. Thus, the Muslim ideal is for the inner peace that comes from confident obedience to Allah to be so strong that death is welcome. Muhammad waged war against the infidels, and all his followers are supposed to follow his lead. Of course, not every Muslim is going to pick up a gun or don a suicide vest, but the teaching is there for those who wish to take a shortcut to Muslim heaven.

Islam has not changed since the seventh century. From its genesis, there has never been distinction between the religious and the political; there has never been hesitation about territorial expansion. Nor have doubts been raised or questions been asked about waging endless war against infidels. Yet, despite Islam's unchanging character, somehow for centuries Europe was able not only to resist the spread of the most aggressive religion that history has ever witnessed but also to keep Islam's painfully ordered and technologically advanced armies at bay.

What has changed between then and now that makes the West no longer able to defend itself against this mortal enemy? Having lived in the West for nine years, I agree with Cardinal Joseph Ratzinger, who in his *Without Roots* explains how the collapse of Western civilization is happening from within, by the turning away from its roots, in other words, the Catholic faith.

Westerners do not seem to appreciate that without religion there can be no culture that contributes to human flourishing. Turkey's case among Muslim countries is somewhat unique, mostly due to Atatürk's secular reforms rather than to an evolution or a process of reformation within Islam. Despite increasing urbanization and secularization, the main aspects of Turkish culture remain deeply Muslim. Young girls need not cover their hair, but the social rules governing female behavior are far more restrictive than those for male behavior. The strength of these norms increases the farther away one travels from urban areas. It is hard to explain to the average Westerner what it means to live in a Muslim society: Islam is not a religion in the way Americans understand the word. It governs every action and seeps into every thought process. It is a religion, yes, but also a political system, a legal system, a social system—in short, a total way of life.

When one departs from this way of life, as I did when I became a Christian, and finds himself a member of a minority group, suddenly the same air that everyone breathes to make the society work becomes toxic. The state of Christians and other minority groups in Muslim countries is well known. It is a daily struggle for Christian converts to remain faithful in such a hostile environment, when one's home becomes unwelcoming and one's relatives and friends become enemies. The pressure is so great that many converts eventually fall away, but the constant fire is purifying for those who remain steadfast.

My first visit to the United States made me feel jealous; a church around every corner with worship bands spoiled by amazing technology, with charismatic pastors who delivered sermons in front of giant screens, with modern hotel-like buildings. It was a dream. Oh, what I would have given up to have this many Christians around me! Surely, I thought, being the follower of such a controversial man as Christ was much easier in America.

Fast forward about four years, when I found myself in England for grad school and about to be confirmed in the Catholic Church. Despite the warnings I received from British and American friends in Turkey, the hope of finally living in a "Christian" country led to an irrational optimism that would soon burst. Once scones, crumpets, and endless cups of tea became a daily routine, the number of teenage mothers on the city buses and the amount of binge drinking in clubs started to make an impact on my perception of the culture. The youth did not gather in a cozy pub for a pint of ale in order to talk about big ideas, as C. S. Lewis and his literary friends did at Oxford. No, they spent hours in bars, losing count of how many drinks they were consuming and hooking up with total strangers for sex. With the legendary English politeness, few of the Catholics I knew talked about the decline of the culture or the state of the youth. Either it was the silence of defeat I was hearing, or I had moved to the land where political correctness had been invented.

In England, I lived in an urban area, surrounded by universities and nightclubs. In the United States, I live in a rural coal town, where my lack of driving skills trapped me until the Department of Homeland Security deemed me worthy of a green card. Again, in my naïveté, the hope of a more Christian, or at least a more wholesome, environment flickered. But I soon discovered that the cherished ideal of rugged individualism did not leave much room for a community whose members truly depend on each other. People were pleasant and much easier to strike up a conversation with than the average Brit, but even in a place where everyone knows each other, people don't ask for help or make much effort to form friendships.

For a long time, I thought I lacked meaningful social interaction because I was a foreigner, but then I realized that growing loneliness and isolation are everybody's problem. I talk to working mothers and stay-at-home mothers, to people from all different backgrounds. Many complain about the lack of true friends. Yet they do not know what to do about it, and the endless hours they spend on social media has not helped them to form bonds with the people who live nearby. Then again, everyone is so busy—there is always a sporting event to cheer, a movie to watch, or a meeting to attend.

Add modern moral relativism to this wonderful concoction of constant input and activity, and the silence on topics of importance becomes deafening. If someone believes—or, God forbid, defends—that there is one ultimate truth that man was created to seek, or that moral choices are either good or bad, heads are shaken and gasps of unbelief are uttered. After being at the receiving end of this reaction enough times, many people choose self-censorship.

I am grateful for the freedoms and the opportunities the United States offers. My children will likely get good educations and grow up to lead prosperous lives. For all of its flaws, America is still the land of equal opportunity, and that promise is the reason so many people idolize life here and so many try to leave their own lands for the shores of this country. Everything that makes the West attractive, however, is a mere echo of its Christian past. When the allure of brand-new cars, spacious houses, and endless entertainments wears off, what does the West have to offer without Christ? Not much, actually. So we should not be surprised that Islam, with its strong identity and community that spring from a shared way of thinking and acting, gains a foothold here and in other Western countries.

Imagine growing up with stark black-and-white rules, not to be bent. Without the flexibility of doubting and the freedom of questioning, Islam offers boundaries and a structure in which to function, which gives a person a sense of security and of his place in the world. Everybody knows what is expected of everybody else. Now imagine moving to the West after years of living in this system. One finds a good job and makes money, but there is nothing beyond the material—there are no rules to live by and nothing is sacred. When he is asked to assimilate, he can just as easily ask: Assimilate into what? There is nothing there in comparison with the strong Muslim community.

When the Ottoman armies raided Europe, despite the sin, the division, and the turmoil, Christ was still the acknowledged Lord of Christendom. How else can anyone explain the Christian victories at Lepanto and Vienna? Sensing that their own identity and culture were in peril, Christian peoples stood not only *against* the enemy that battered the gates in the East but *for* their cherished faith. They will need to do so again.

21

Discovering the Joy
of Spreading the Faith

When I finished my dissertation after many long years and too many revisions, my husband and I already had two children. At that time, the thought of staying at home to take care of our children was not even on my radar. Our children were small, and life with them looked boring and bleak. I thought I would surely go out of my mind changing all those diapers and singing "Five Little Monkeys" thirty times a day. I applied for a few positions, got rejected, and stamped my foot. Yet through it all, the Lord was trying to show me that the hands-on mothering work in front of me was much more valuable to Him than the intellectual work I kept fantasizing about doing. One day during Adoration, I finally said to the Lord, "Thy will be done." The words had not come easily, but once I finally uttered them wholeheartedly, once I truly surrendered myself to the Lord, the freedom and the sense of relief that followed were overwhelming.

That turning point was four years ago, and since then Virgil and I have had two more children. Being a stay-at-home mother is harder now, but my sense of purpose is clearer than when I first began. Yes, I still struggle with isolation, loneliness, and too many insipid children's songs. Unsurprisingly, my study of American foreign policy did not teach me what to do when a two-year-old poops in the bathtub or when a four-year-old stuffs his ears with blue Play-Doh. Many a time during the day, I am glad that I have thick hair, because the occasions for pulling my hair out are frequent. The mess is so persistent that I can't even call myself a housewife, because the house might beg to differ. There are always dirty dishes in the sink, and I am sure that some troll keeps getting our clothes dirty, because there is always a mountain of laundry. Holding a sick toddler and letting him vomit in my hair, hoping that none of the vomit will get on the floor, is not unheard of because neither is thinking that washing my hair in the shower is much easier than trying to get the puke out of the carpet.

Then, when my little girl runs to me and gives my leg a big hug, yelling "Mummy", or when my big boy plays with my hair while drinking his milk as he sits in my lap, all the trivial worries of housekeeping melt away. I think about the hours, days, and months spent working on my dissertation and realize that the satisfaction of having a doc-torate does not even come close to the joy of hearing "I love you" from one of my children. Nothing I have done or will ever do in this life will be as important as caring for these tiny people and their eternal souls. I understand now that even if I had believed that only women who work outside the home are happy and that stay-at-home moms are oppressed by the shackles of sexism and patriarchy, I would have been miserable working all day long in an office far from my children. Such a life was not my calling, and the Lord knew me much better than I knew myself.

As accepting as I am with my current season in life, I am sometimes deeply troubled. Not long after the birth of our third child, I was lying awake, staring at a crucifix on the wall. It was four in the morning and the house was quiet, but sleep eluded me as I kept thinking about the upcoming Synod on the Family. With my postpartum tendency to hysteria, the rumors about how the Catholic understanding of marriage might be altered by the synod were too loud for me to ignore.

"If they change the definition of marriage at this synod, how can I believe You?" I asked Christ's crucified body.

"Lord, there is nowhere else for me to go. If You can't keep Your word, what kind of a God are You?" I asked again, but the slain Son of God still did not answer.

"You promised," I said finally and got up to answer the cry of my newborn. I put the binky back into his mouth and admired how perfect he was even when he managed to scream a lot louder than his size would suggest was possible. "You promised," I whispered once more, staring at one of the undeserved blessings He gave me.

That night of desperation has stuck with me to this day. It was one of many moments of weakness when I put my trust in men, rather than in God. In the following months, as more confusion was blown around by the media, I reminded myself that the Creator of the universe is capable of keeping His promises. These times we are living in, and every other tumultuous era before ours, are nothing but parentheses in the eternal scheme of God.

Just as during other dark times, the Lord is asking for the cooperation of His people, who have been given extraordinary graces through His Church. Christianity in Western societies has been watered down by indifference and weakened by relativism. Christians are scorned by those in government, media, and education who think that believing in anything other than what their death culture suggests is bigotry. In many places throughout the world, Christians are killed, tortured, and imprisoned without a whisper. Thus, the question we must ask ourselves is, "What can I do to change the tide?"

I was listening to a wisdom-packed episode of *Kresta in the Afternoon* as I drove my children to a fancy playground. In the middle of the children's singing "Let It Go" from the Disney film *Frozen*, Mr. Kresta asked his radio audience what they did for the kingdom of God. I don't know whether he used those exact words, but the image that came to mind was of each and every one of us sitting on a treasure that would multiply if only we would share it. Not long after that podcast, I decided to write this conversion story, not only for my children, but also for anyone who would be inspired by it. If this book sparks a light in one person's soul, the months of writing, waiting, and editing will be more than worth it. Consider what would happen if millions of us shared our treasures.

I know how easy it is to blame the decades of secularization for the vanishing Christian culture and the dwindling numbers of faithful. But we must resist the temptation to look back and to point fingers. Instead we must strive to give future generations a more faithful, more on-fire, and more attractive Church.

There is much that each one of us can do regardless of who we are, where we live, or how much time we have.

Learn the Faith

We are not the illiterate masses who relied on wandering monks and priests to teach us our faith. I love seeing monks and nuns clad in their distinctive habits, and it would be wonderful if my children could be around more of them. But, even then, we would still have an obligation to learn the faith for ourselves, to share it with others, and to teach it to our children. Can any of us use the excuse "I didn't know" when there is so much Catholic information available both online and in print? Listen to podcasts; read one article a day; get a subscription to a Catholic magazine; go to a conference. If you do one little thing each week, imagine how much you can learn in a year.

Feeding the mind the right food affects every aspect of life. I don't know where my faith would be if I hadn't read *The Apostasy That Wasn't*, which showed me that there was much martyrdom and heresy as well as many faithful and holy men even in the fourth century. I don't know where my parenting would be if I didn't listen to Dr. Ray's podcasts, which help me to navigate through the fog of modern psychology. I don't know how familiar I would be with apologetics, bioethics, or even movies if I didn't frequent Catholic Answers or read books on the faith and faithful living. The more I feed my mind, especially when I feel alone and in despair, the more my emotional responses are tamed by my reason.

Pray, Pray, Pray

Then, of course, pray more.

As I said before, praying doesn't come easy to me, but I have gotten better over the years. After all, what's the point of believing in God if you don't have regular conversations with Him, with His Mother, and with the other people in communion with Him, the saints?

My husband has a great devotion to the Rosary, and he prays all the mysteries every day. His devotion has inspired me greatly. Thanks to his example, when I feel angry, depressed, or even under the weather, I pray a Rosary. More often than not, it is the background to the tedious chores of the day, as we bought a recording of the Rosary to listen to when our hands are busy.

Over the years I have tried to memorize common prayers. One of the most efficient ways for me to do so is to print the prayers out, stick them on the bathroom wall, and read them aloud every morning. Before long, my memory retains the words.

Lastly, I try to talk to God, instead of running meaningless conversations, really monologues, in my head. After all, I do not have much wisdom to offer myself. Mental prayer not only takes me out of my own limited world, but also keeps the communication line with God open.

One final and crucial aspect of prayer is that it offers protection against the devil and his attacks. It would be naïve and irresponsible to deny the work of Satan in the culture of death, in the Church, and even in our own lives. We must equip ourselves not only with sacraments and sacramentals but with daily prayer. Going to Adoration and reciting a prayer to Saint Michael the Archangel are good places to start.

Prayer, like all things that are worth doing well, requires practice. Even though I am far from being a woman of prayer, that bridge between heaven and earth has saved my sanity, protected me, and brought me closer to God. Despite the frequency of my failures, I strive to be on my knees as often as I can.

Tithe

I quickly learned in Catholic circles that tithing is not a very popular topic. Once a year, the typical parish priest gives the obligatory money talk, and most of his parishioners dutifully ignore it. Our Protestant brethren are much better at this than we are, and thanks to them, I was committed to tithing long before I crossed the threshold of a Catholic church.

Giving is not only for the receiver. In my personal life and in my marriage, I have seen the amazing blessings that come from sharing a little bit of what God has given us. Materialism is one of the biggest blinders the current culture slaps on our faces. When we set aside God's share of our income, before we spend it on anything else, not only do we put our trust in something other than our jobs, but also we realize month by month that there are more important things in life than getting the best and the newest of everything.

My one-income family of six can surely use the 10 percent we set aside for Church and charity, but that small amount reminds us that all we have is from the Lord, for us to use according to His will. It also keeps our eyes open to others' needs and provides the means to help others when we see those needs. Tithing undoubtedly is one of the most difficult and most rewarding things we do as a family, reminding us time and time again to trust and to remember that comforting verse: "And why are you anxious about clothing? Consider the lilies of the field, how they grow; they neither toil nor spin; yet I tell you, even Solomon in all his glory was not clothed like one of these" (Mt 6:28–29).

Be a Living Thing

G. K. Chesterton said in *The Everlasting Man*: "A dead thing can go with the stream, but only a living thing can go against it."[1] I have tried to describe the stream we live in with its strong current, its muddy waters, and its dead or dying fish

---

[1] G. K. Chesterton, *The Everlasting Man* (San Francisco: Ignatius Press, 1993), p. 256.

that float by. We Christians are living things because of our life in Christ. We therefore have the tools and the graces to swim against the current and, we hope, to help other fish to find the source of life. How do we do that? The task is different for every one of us, but it can be summed up by a line from the movie *Robots*: "See a need, fill a need." In our daily lives—in our families, parishes, and workplaces—there are always needs. The ones we are called to fill will be different for all of us, but none are trivial. No act is too small. As Mother Teresa often said, we cannot do great things. We can only do small things with great love.

Because of Christ's love and mercy, every day I strive to travel onward and upward in faith and to find ways to share my faith. More often than not, I fall, but then there is always more forgiveness, more graces, and more love to pick me back up. If all those years ago, the whisper of grace had not become loud enough for me to hear and to follow, I don't know where I would be today. I certainly would not have learned to love and be loved unconditionally.

I would love to hop into TARDIS and travel back in time to have a chat with my twenty-year-old self, telling her that in seventeen years she would be Catholic, married to an American, raising four children, and writing on the side. She would not believe it. She would more readily believe in a time machine and an alien race with two hearts than in the version of herself that I have become.

It occurs to me that little by little, I traveled far.

It occurs to me that God is forever faithful.

It occurs to me that I was lost, but now I am found.